STAY GROOVY

WHERE HUMOR MEETS THE SOUL

R.W. WESELY

BEFORE YOU BEGIN

What you're about to read exists because a few brave souls told me, "You really should write this stuff down." So here it is—thanks to those kind (and persistent) encouragers.

The stories appear in the order they popped into my brain. There's no grand design. No hidden code. No secret map to buried treasure. Don't try to make sense of it—just read, relax, and (I hope) laugh or cry.

These stories are drawn from the life of the author, R.W. Wesley—known to friends and family as Bob (or Bobby) Niemond.

HEALTH ADVISORY

Recent clinical studies* suggest that reading these stories while drinking milk may result in:

- **Snortelosis™** —A rare but spectacular phenomenon involving the unexpected evacuation of milk through the nostrils.

- **Sudden Oxygen Deprivation**—Triggered by uncontrollable wheezing, gasping, or making that awkward seal-bark laugh you thought you'd outgrown.

- **Public Embarrassment**—Often accompanied by the dreaded phrase: "Cleanup on aisle three."

- **Unplanned Device Replacement**—Because apparently, laptops and dairy-based beverages don't mix.

**(Okay, no actual studies were conducted. But still—don't say we didn't warn you.)*

1

PACIFIC PALISADES

This is for anyone out there who thinks growing up in Pacific Palisades was some sort of breezy utopia where we floated around on inflatable swans in infinity pools while butlers misted us with mineral water. Let me shatter that delusion right now: it was a *war zone.*

I walked home from Marquez Elementary School. *Every. Single. Day.* It wasn't just a stroll—it was a full-blown saga that spanned several grueling years. My daily trek home wasn't a walk; it was a test of human endurance.

I faced punishing mid-70s heat waves, froze in the glacial chill of the low 70s, and on the worst days? High 70s. Sweltering. *I practically evaporated.* You think you've experienced struggle? Try trudging through a light marine layer. It's like nature's way of saying, "Don't get cocky." And sometimes, it was *overcast.* Do you know what it's like to not even have your shadow to guide you? SPF 50 wasn't optional—it was survival gear.

And don't let Google lie to you. They'll try to tell you it was only 0.8 miles from Marquez to my house on Pequeno Place. *Lies!* How is that even possible! I took *five* streets to get home. It was at least 18 miles, minimum. Uphill. Both ways. I'd get home *after my dad arrived from work* to a cold dinner and the theme song from *Perry Mason* seared into my brain. Google Maps also conveniently forgets to factor in Lachman Lane—aka *Satan's Staircase.* That hill wasn't just steep; it was vertical. I'm convinced they shot scenes from *Cliffhanger* there. You needed ropes, harnesses, and a sherpa just to make it to the top. No wonder I felt like planting the American flag when I walked in the door each night around 9:30 p.m.

And don't even get me started on Pequeno Place. "Pequeno" means small, but living there felt like crossing the Sahara every time I stepped outside. If Fitbits had existed, mine would've exploded halfway up Lachman.

Now, let's talk about the Alice's. We lived on Pequeno Place, a street so steep that it had switchback sidewalks. Alice S. lived above me—literally above me. I'm convinced she was seven feet tall. The woman had the wingspan of a California condor. Yet, no basketball scholarship? A missed opportunity for Team USA. Alice, if you're out there, please confirm your height because it was awe-inspiring.

Additionally, she sported a beautiful smile. But when you're busy trying not to flunk fourth grade, there's no time for smiles, no matter how tall or pretty. In addition to the academic rigors of fourth grade, I had hall monitor duties to fulfill. You try learning addition while spending most of your time guarding the door... from the outside... all day!

Then there was Alice G. She dressed up as a Campbell's Tomato Soup can for Halloween. Not once. *Twice.* It was a bold fashion statement. Alice, if you're reading this, please confirm it wasn't a fever dream. I need to know.

But my greatest hardship at Marquez wasn't academic purgatory in fourth grade. Oh no. It was the eternal shame of being the only A6 team captain to lose to B6 in kickball. *Kickball.* A game so simple it's basically "soccer for people who don't like moving." And yet, we lost. Why? Because fate is cruel, and if I remember correctly, Kyle was blinded by the sun bouncing off the glint of the tin foil wrapper on Alice's costume, allowing the winning run to score. Alice, again, please verify or deny—I need closure.

So don't tell me we had it easy in the Palisades. Sure, it wasn't exactly *Oliver Twist*, but it wasn't all rainbows and artisanal kale either.

If the utter devastation caused by the fires taught us anything, it's that you can burn the buildings, but you can't burn the memories. And for better or worse, mine include tin-foil soup cans, gravity-defying smiles, and my tragic kickball legacy.

Alice—seriously. Verify.

~

THERE ARE three lessons to learn from my incredibly difficult childhood:

1. Never trust Google Maps. If it says 0.8 miles, it's lying. Add at least 17 bonus miles for character development, marine layers, and vertical sidewalks. That's just science.

2. If someone dresses up as a soup can for Halloween more than once, don't question it—just draft them early for your kickball team. And position them away from the sun's reflection. Preferably behind a wall.

3. Life may feel uphill both ways, but grace means someone already made it to the top on your behalf. You just have to follow.

— Stay Groovy

2

MARQUEZ ELEMENTARY SCHOOL

If there was ever a poster boy for ADHD, I was it. I would have been their national spokesperson. Fidgety doesn't even scratch the surface. I was like a hummingbird who'd just snorted Pixy Stix. The fact that other people could sit still totally baffled me. Were they aliens? Superheroes? Had they been secretly glued to their chairs?

I still vividly recall Ms. McAllister, in her saintly tone, addressing the class: "Everyone, please sit silently with folded hands."

Naturally, I leaned over to Denny, who was sitting silently with folded hands, and asked, "How do you even *do* that?" Boom. Five seconds in, I'd broken two cardinal rules: (1) silence and (2) folded hands. Efficiency at its finest. A two-for-one master class in classroom disruption. And so, I was sent to "continue my conversation outside," which I guess was teacher code for "go be someone else's problem." Of course, the real issue? No one *joined me* out there. *Continue the conversation with whom?* It was just me, a lone exile, mulling over life's mysteries like, "Why are cafeteria hot dogs *so* shiny?"

Talking wasn't just a habit for me; it was a *destiny*. A calling, really. I wasn't disruptive—I was *practicing* for my future career as a public speaker. You'd think someone would have recognized this raw talent and that one day I would fall back on these techniques as a pastor. But nooo, all I got was, "Bobby, please continue the conversation outside."

On one memorable day, I preemptively stood up as the teacher said, "Bobby..." and held up a hand like a traffic cop and said, "Say no more," then strutted out. Honestly, I should've left with, "Thank you, I'll be here all week" in my best Elvis drawl. Missed opportunity.

By this point, I had a PhD in "U notices." The moment the teacher approached, I'd casually raise my hand to accept mine like I was collecting a trophy. The "lacks self-control" box? Oh, that was my *spotlight.* Sometimes the checkmarks were so intense, it looked like the teacher had been possessed by an angry seismograph. The paper wasn't just marked—it was *traumatized.* I half expected to hear it whisper, "Help me," as it crumpled under the sheer force of frustration. Was this really about me, or did the teachers just need therapy?

And then came fifth grade. Enter Ms. Parnel, a teacher so amazing, she might as well have descended from the clouds with wings. She didn't just see a fidgety distraction tornado; she saw *potential.* One day, after reading a letter from my mom (probably apologizing for raising a human pogo stick), Ms. Parnel did something miraculous: she hugged me. Not in a "I m 'm-giving-up-on-you" way, but in a "Hey, you're worth something" way.

Let me tell you, that hug hit me like a lightning bolt. Suddenly, I wanted to do well. *Me!* The class clown turned hallway wanderer. I started skipping "U notices." The other kids were *shaken.* "Wait, Bobby didn't get a U notice? Is... is the earth reversing its rotation?"

Nope, just me realizing that someone believed in me.

Which prepared me for...sixth grade.

Mr. Cranefield, a bald enigma, had two trademarks: (1) saying "clear as mud," which confused me endlessly (mud isn't clear, Mr. Cranefield—*that's why it's called mud*) and (2) slamming a yardstick on his desk so loudly it could wake the dead. The first time it happened, I thought we were under attack. But no—it was just his way of firmly but lovingly saying, "Focus, you little hooligans."

Except, of course, Alice G. She never needed focusing. Alice G.

was *perfect.* She didn't even breathe loudly. The rest of us were practically feral, but Alice? She floated through life like she was auditioning for sainthood. Ugh, the GLINT issue rises again.

STILL, between Ms. Parnel's hug and Mr. Cranefield's desk-slapping vigilance, I learned some important life lessons:

1. Bald men with rulers are not to be trifled with.

2. If not addressed with therapy, a single GLINT issue can apparently last a lifetime.

3. One small act of kindness—like a hug—can transform a kid's trajectory. So, if you ever meet a fifth grader, hug them. Not in a creepy way. Just enough to let them know you believe in them. Because sometimes, all it takes to turn a "lacks self-control" kid into a success story is someone who sees the best in them. Or, at least into someone who writes humorous self-deprecating stories.

— Stay Groovy

3

THE MILK TRUCK

The following set of articles is titled "Do You Remember When...?"—a whimsical mix of historical confusion, nostalgic absurdity, and a Calvin-like imagination. Enjoy!

Do You Remember When...? #1

...Milk was delivered by truck? Shane does. Oh, Shane remembers *everything.* Before I explain our brilliant strategy, you need to understand our milkman's route. Picture a giant teardrop—long line leading in, loop around, long line leading out the same direction as the line in. The crucial rule: *Jump off before the truck leaves the loop.* Otherwise, you're not just going around the block—you're taking the Milk Truck Express to the far reaches of the galaxy.

Now, I know you think you know where this is going. Trust me. You don't.

Now, our little gang—Kyle, Kade, and me—had this down to an art. We were eleven, maybe twelve. Pros. Veterans of the milk truck rodeo. Enter Shane, Kade's six-year-old brother. Why Kade thought Shane should come along that day remains a mystery. Shane was a newbie. A rookie in a league of seasoned professionals. This was not "bring your little brother to chaos day." What kind of seasoned stunt crew lets a toddler on board? But there he was, all eager-eyed and clutching his juice box.

The plan was simple: Hide behind trash cans (thank you, Tuesday trash day), jump on the back of the truck as it pulled away, ride a few houses down, jump off, and vanish like dairy-loving ghosts. The best part? The driver: Mr. Fussy Pants. He was already mad about life. And he was becoming angrier by the stop as we scampered off and on. You could see it in the way he slammed milk bottles down like he was punishing the universe for inventing lactose. I half-expected him to start hurling milk bottles like grenades.

Things were going great—until they weren't.

See, Shane wasn't *grasping* the whole "jump off" part of the game. We warned him—*repeatedly*. "Shane, if you don't jump off at the next stop, you'll end up riding the truck to the ends of the earth." He nodded solemnly, like he understood. But spoiler alert: He did *not* understand.

The critical moment came. We jumped off like the milk truck commandos we were. Shane? Shane froze. He clung to the truck. Eyes wide. Mouth open. Absolute terror plastered across his face. It was tragic—and frankly, hilarious at the same time. It was Shane. The truck sped off. Shane hanging on for dear life, headed straight for the edge of the known world (aka Culver City).

Now, I know what you're thinking: *Did we chase the truck? Did we call for help? Did we panic?* The answer is... sort of. We waited a full minute before shrugging it off and began playing hide-and-seek. Hey, we were kids.

Shane, on the other hand, stayed on that truck for what felt like an eternity. Seven hours later, when the driver finally parked, Shane bolted. I don't know how far he ran, but rumor has it he crossed state lines.

Here's where it gets weird. According to local legend, Shane was adopted by the family who found him and later earned a PhD Laramie State with a groundbreaking dissertation on why cows always face the same direction in a field. Today, Shane lectures internationally, often starting his presentations with the phrase, "It all began with a milk truck..." A Wyoming success story, really.

Now, here's the twist. Shane wasn't *actually* lost. He was erased. Yep, Kyle and Kade managed to convince their little sister Mallory that Shane was imaginary. And anytime their mom asked about Shane, they'd run upstairs and shout, "He's up here!" Chaos ensued, and with four kids in the house that felt like eight, nobody questioned it.

To this day, Mallory probably thinks Shane was a figment of her imagination. Mallory, if you're reading this, our bad.

This story is only being released because Kyle and Kade are now safely enrolled in the witness protection program.

And Mr. Fussy Pants? He retired and moved to a remote region of the Yukon and lived off-grid, and didn't speak for nine years.

As for Shane, he's doing fine. He doesn't drink milk anymore though. Too many bad memories.

~

IF THIS STORY leaves us with anything, it's this:

1. If you don't jump off in time you might end up with a PhD in cows.

2. Never let your younger brother tag along unless you're okay erasing him from the family records.

3. Sometimes, even when you think you're lost, forgotten, or hanging on for dear life, the ride might be leading you exactly where you were meant to be all along.

— Stay Groovy

4

BATMAN

We interrupt the "Do You Remember When...?" series for this urgent Bat-message.

This is a story about Batman. Or at least, it was supposed to be about Batman. But before we dive into the tights and Batmobiles, we need to address something critical: the misuse of *The* when talking about Pacific Palisades.

National news anchors always say, "*The* Pacific Palisades," like it's some exclusive, gated community where only retired superheroes live. No, no, NO. Locals just say, "Pacific Palisades" or, if you're cool, "The Palisades." You only slap a "The" on it when you're acting like it's the center of the universe—which, by the way, it totally is.

And while we're at it, can we talk about Pacific Palisades Charter High School? Five words? Really? Nobody called it that. It was Pali High. Or just Pali. The word *charter* was as unnecessary as putting ketchup on a steak. So, stop it!

But I digress.

Focus, Bobby. FOCUS.

(That phrase, by the way, was practically my childhood slogan. If I'd had a family crest, it would've been a wide-eyed squirrel on a Red Bull binge, surrounded by the words *FOCUS, Bobby. FOCUS.*)

Anyway. Batman. Let's go.

Growing up in The Palisades—and yes, note the correct use of *The*—wasn't as glamorous as people think. Sure, Adam West, the actual Batman, lived there. No big deal. He even sat in my section at a local restaurant, where I was a waiter. However, saying, "Thank you, citizen," was a bit too much in character for a guy who made his living wearing tights and a funny hat with small pointy ears. Relax, dude. You're eating lasagna, not foiling The Joker.

But this isn't about Adam West, the person. It's about the show. You know, the classic "dadadadadadadadadada BATMAN" one. If you didn't just sing that in your head, are you even human?

But it wasn't all capes and grappling hooks. For example, growing up my family only had a black-and-white TV. BLACK. AND. WHITE. You ever try watching Batman without color? It's like eating cereal without milk—technically possible, but why even bother?

Thankfully, salvation came in the form of Mike and Ryan, who lived down the street and had a glorious technicolor TV. Every Thursday at 7:30 p.m., on the same Bat-channel, the neighborhood kids would descend on their house like moths to a porch light. You had to watch Batman in color. Without it, the POWS, SOCKS, and BAMS were just sad little noises on a grayscale screen.

Now, picture this: five hyperactive boys crammed onto a couch, all jittery with anticipation. The iconic fight scene begins—POW! BAM! WHACK!—and suddenly, we're not just watching Batman. Oh no. We become Batman. Pillows start flying. Couch cushions are weaponized. Somebody (who might or might not have been me) decides it's time to scale the furniture like Spider-Man (wrong superhero, but whatever). The living room transforms into a full-blown battlefield.

I distinctly remember that person (okay, me) midair, spread-eagle, about to use all of his sixty-seven pounds to extinguish evil when...

...Mrs. G. appears.

"WHAT IS THIS... THIS...?" she roars, her voice so powerful I'm pretty sure it triggered car alarms up and down the street.

The TV goes dark. The chaos screeches to a halt. We all freeze, mid-pillow-throw, as she delivers the dreaded double "THIS."

(Pro tip: When a mom has to say "this" twice, run!)

"I WILL NOT HAVE THIS... THIS... IN MY HOUSE!" she continues, each word dripping with righteous fury.

And just like that, we were banished.

Out we went, single file, heads hanging like criminals shuffling off to jail.

Mike and Ryan stayed behind, sentenced to their rooms, while the rest of us wandered into the night. After a few houses, Kyle and Kade peeled off to their home, and I shuffled off into the evening mist, still trying to process what had just happened.

Didn't Mrs. G understand that we were helping Batman? That Gotham—or at least Pacific Palisades—needed us to channel our inner heroes?

Apparently not.

When I got home, my mom asked why I was back so early.

Still dazed, I muttered, "This... this," and retreated to my room, where I spent the rest of the night using action figures to reenact the battle we'd started. Evil wouldn't rest until next Thursday, so neither would I.

Years later, I realized what I should've told my mom: "Honestly, we deserved it. The G family is classy and respectable. More importantly, quiet and reserved. I don't know what we were thinking. Bad read of the room, Mom. We turned their living room into WWE: Batman Edition. Mrs. G was right to shut us down."

~

But at age ten, self-reflection wasn't in my skill set. The only thing I knew was this:

1. Watching Batman in black and white is a crime against humanity.

2. Moms with "THIS... THIS" energy are not to be trifled with.

3. And, most importantly, when the POWS and BAMS fade and the laugh track cuts out, someone still has to stand. Because even when you've been exiled from color-TV paradise, Gotham still needs its heroes—especially the ones who rise when the world thinks the credits have already rolled.

— Stay Groovy

5

DRIVER'S ED

Do You Remember When...? #2

...Driver's Ed was an actual high school class? Back when the state of California, in its infinite wisdom, decided that fifteen-year-olds—whose decision-making skills hovered somewhere between a caffeinated squirrel and a toddler with a set of car keys—should be entrusted with moving vehicles... for *academic credit*?

Thank God for that instructor-side brake pedal. Because let me tell you, that thing saved my life.

The Chaos Begins: The Simulators

Ah, the "simulators."

A collection of ancient arcade machines repurposed for suffering, where we sat in fake cars watching a grainy 1970s instructional film that looked like it had been shot by someone with a personal vendetta against autofocus.

Naturally, we thought it would be hilarious to test the limits of the machine by violently spinning the wheel and flooring the accelerator, doing virtual donuts like we'd just won the Indy 500.

Our instructor, however, had long since lost patience for nonsense. One day, when we're all in peak giggle mode, he reached over, grabbed a stack of metal film cans, and *launched* them down the aisle like he was summoning an ancient demon.

The sound? Deafening.

The effect? Immediate cardiac trauma.

Pretty sure my arrhythmia started right then and there.

The Real Car: Entering the Danger Zone

Fast forward to the actual car—a drab yellow Ford Fairlane. You'd think they'd start us off easy. Maybe a quick tutorial on which pedal makes it go and which pedal makes it stop before tossing us onto the streets of Los Angeles.

Nope. Apparently, they assumed we absorbed *all* that from the simulators.

Which, to be clear, we absolutely did not.

Except Alice G.

Oh, I'm *sure* she did.

But the rest of us? No clue.

And yet, here we were, flung into LA traffic—a trial so intense it made medieval duels look like reasonable conflict resolution.

The car starts. Everything seems fine... until the instructor casually remarks: "So, who is Maggie?"

Enter Greg

Greg was a legend. We loved asking Greg what he did over the weekend because Greg—God bless him—was *pathologically honest.*

His stories weren't exaggerated. They weren't even bragging. He just *told it like it was.*

And yes, the LAPD was usually involved, but always in a Keystone Cops kind of way.

This is the same Greg who:

- Spray-painted *"I ♥ MAGGIE"* on the admin building in letters large enough to be seen from outer space.
- Walked into class the following morning wearing the same paint-splattered shoes from the crime scene.
- Saw two LAPD detectives enter, panicked, and *hurled his shoes into a cabinet*—where they remained for *months.*

Yes. *That* Greg.

(He's fine, by the way. I checked. Statute of limitations ran out.)

THE INFAMOUS ROUTE: A Disaster in Four Parts

Our first driving route was a box route with four drivers, each taking a one-mile leg.

What could possibly go wrong?

LEG 1: Easy Peasy

First student: Drive straight down Temescal Canyon Drive. A little weaving, but mission accomplished. No casualties. No property damage. We felt hopeful.

LEG 2: Pacific Coast Highway

New driver takes over. So far, so good, but I'd like to personally question the genius who thought letting a first-time driver navigate PCH was a *good* idea.

Amazingly, we completed PCH without mishap.

Two drivers down, two to go. *Maybe this won't be so bad.*

Wrong.

I was supposed to be Driver #4. Sunset back to Pali. Flat. Easy. Fun.

It never happened.

. . .

LEG 3: The Baja 1000 in Four Minutes

An uphill narrow winding, two lane road.

The driver for Leg 3: *Benny*

Thin. Mild-mannered. Good student. Glasses. Long black hair he occasionally whipped back.

Nothing about him suggested that, within minutes, we'd be at AUTOMOTIVE DEFCON 1.

At first, Benny was fine. But then...

35 MPH—A little fast, but nothing crazy.

40 MPH—Hmm. Maybe ease up, buddy.

45...50...55 MPH—Okay, what is happening?

At this point, we start side-eyeing each other. "Uh... is Benny good?"

Benny was *not* good.

I glance up. Benny has a white-knuckle grip on the wheel. His hands are at the prescribed ten and two, but his arms are locked. He steers by rocking side to side. Pretty sure *that* isn't prescribed. His teeth? *Clenched.* He breathing? He's *PANTING! Loudly.*

60... 65... 70 MPH— Now everyone is screaming:

"BENNY, SLOW DOWN!!!"

When *adults* scream, you know it's serious.

75 MPH—I make eye contact with Benny in the mirror.

His eyes are glazed. He's *GONE.*

80 MPH—The car feels like Apollo 13 reentering Earth's atmosphere.

Violent shaking. Rising heat. Deafening noise. Flames flash horizontally across the windows because of the velocity.

Thank God for that instructor-side brake pedal. But Benny was *also* pressing the accelerator, which left us in a sadistic game of "Who Can Press Harder?"

Ever heard what happens when the accelerator and brake pedal are both slammed to the floor at the same time?

Neither had we.

It's a very loud mechanical argument where the car can't decide whether to implode or explode—so instead, it just sits there screaming in existential crisis.

It's the automotive equivalent of trying to run a marathon with your shoelaces tied together while juggling flaming torches and being chased by an angry goose—but louder and with way more collateral damage.

Trust me, you don't want to hear that. But if you do, you'll never un-hear it.

Finally, the instructor reached over, *turned the key off*, and the car *crawled* to a halt—gently coming to rest against the back bumper of one of those blue mass transit buses.

THE AFTERMATH: *Survival Mode*

We sat in stunned silence.

One by one, we stumbled out, gathered on the sidewalk, and stared at:

- Benny, still in the driver's seat, frozen in place. Panting.
- The instructor, in shock but muttering to himself: "I should've been a plumber."
- The car, wheezing like an asthmatic, smelling of shame and despair.

Needless to say, *I never got to drive that day.*

BUT LIKE ALL OF LIFE, there are lessons to be learned. Mine were:

1. I used to think instructors had those extra brake pedals just in case. Nope. That thing is the only reason half of us didn't take out a mailbox, shopping cart, or an entire Arby's.

2. Life is about perspective. Greg saw the world differently. Where we saw rules, he saw suggestions. And where we saw a reasonable speed limit, Benny saw an opportunity to break the sound barrier.

3. Sometimes, we speed through life, blind to the dangers ahead, until a well-timed brake pedal intervenes—saving us from a disaster we never even saw coming, keeping us from burning up in low Earth orbit.

— Stay Groovy

6

HELM'S BAKERY TRUCK

Do you remember when...? #3

...Donuts were delivered by the Helms Bakery Truck?

Do you remember when donuts weren't just a drive-thru afterthought but a life-altering event that arrived on wheels? Enter the Helms Bakery Truck—if we can even call it a truck.

What *was* that thing, anyway? It looked like a rolling yellow box with a blue roof. And the sound? A high-pitched, panicked train whistle that sounded like it was being held hostage.

To us, however, it was the mating call of Saturday morning, and the moment we heard it, we moved like Olympic sprinters toward the street.

But honestly, did the design or sound even matter? That truck could've been painted hot pink with My Little Pony decals, and I still would have chased it down barefoot, in my Scooby-Doo pajamas, like a sugar-crazed lunatic.

The Holy Ritual of Donut Selection

The process was sacred. The Helms driver wasn't moody Mr. Fussy Pants—he was the high priest of pastries, welcoming us into his cathedral of confections: the lacquered wood-paneled interior, the polished brass handles, the heavenly aroma of fresh-baked perfection.

And then, the moment of truth as he slid open the wooden drawers with the grace of a Broadway stagehand pulling up the curtain, revealing tray after tray of sugary divinity: the carbohydrate jewelry case, where diamonds came glazed, powdered, or custard-filled.

But the bold move—the choice of legends, the one that separated the casual snacker from the true connoisseur—was, if you're honest with yourself, the only logical decision: the chocolate bar.

This wasn't just a donut. It was an engineering marvel. It took up the most real estate and had enough sugar to power a kindergarten class for three days. Which meant it got me through noon.

But there was one small issue: Timing.

The Saturday Morning Cartoon Dilemma

See, in those days, we had no DVR, pause button, or rewind. If you missed something, it was gone forever—lost to the void of time.

And me? I was in serious danger of missing a single millisecond of the most important show of my young life...

That's right. Johnny. Freakin'. Quest!

Each episode was a masterclass in suspense:

- Will Johnny escape the clutches of evil?
- Will Bandit bark at the wrong time and ruin everything?
- Will Hadji unleash his next-level genius again?

These were critical questions. Life-altering questions.

If I miscalculated my donut retrieval speed, I risked missing a crucial scene and being permanently out of the loop.

This, my friends, was high-stakes decision-making.

. . .

My Credentials in Cartoon Science

Now, you may be wondering, *Bobby, how do you know so much about cartoons?*

Glad you asked.

I hold a PhD in Cartoonology from the prestigious University of Southern Crete (USC).

Yeah, I, too, thought it was that other USC. But once I saw the academic rigor—which involved watching hour upon hour of cartoons—I knew I had found my calling.

And now, after years of exhaustive research (*and zero real-world application*), I present to you...

The Definitive, Scientifically Proven, Academically Tested, Top-Tier Cartoons:

1. *The Flintstones*

If you don't hear "Flintstones, meet the Flintstones" in your head right now, congratulations, you're a liar.

This theme song is so deeply burned into our collective memory that it's impossible to remove.

Warning: If you sing it, you will be stuck with it for seventy-two hours, minimum.

Bonus if you can complete the phrase: "*Yabba-dabba-____*" Double points if you can name both couples and the town they lived in.

2. Wile E. Coyote & Road Runner

Top Four Reasons This Show Is a Masterpiece:

- The explosions. There was one every four minutes, which was perfect for my ADHD.
- The suspense. Every week, I believed the Road Runner could finally get caught.
- The engineering. How does an animal with no opposable

thumbs build functioning rocket launchers out of Acme catalogs?
- Resiliency. The Road Runner has no real abilities except speed and a two-word vocabulary ("Meep, Meep")—yet he outsmarts a coyote with an unlimited budget.

The Next Level Cartoons

1. *George of the Jungle*

A one-season wonder that remains a cult classic.

Had a theme song so catchy, you just started singing it in your head. Admit it.

George, George, George of the Jungle, friend to you and me, WATCH OUT FOR THAT—!

...Tree. You knew it was coming.

2. *The Jetsons*

I wanted to like it. I really did.

But every episode was filled with future technology that seemed ridiculous and impossible.

Flying cars? A push-button home? A robot maid? Yeah right.

(Excuse me: "Alexa, turn off my lights.")

The Cartoons That Left Me Deeply Confused

1. *Courageous Cat and Minute Mouse*

First question: What is a Minute Mouse?

Second question: Why is a cat courageous?

Cats are not courageous. They are moody, judgmental, and disapproving.

This was a lie.

2. *The Herculoids*

First thought: *What does this remind you of?* Yup, me too.

Second thought: *How did a show that starts with H and ends with "oids" ever think it could captivate five-to-nine-year-olds?*

Final thought: *Who was the executive who thought a show a few letters away from a medical condition was a good idea?*

Life Lessons & Unsolved Mysteries

1. When donuts are involved, marketing doesn't matter. The Helms Bakery Truck's whistle wasn't just a sound—it was a Pavlovian trigger that sent kids hurtling barefoot over hedges like gazelles because nothing—not shoes, common sense, or even pants—was more important than securing a donut the size of your head.

2. The mystery may never be solved. We all instantly recall what Fred Flintstone yelled when his saber-toothed cat threw him out of the house ("WILMAAAAAA!")—but ask us what we had for dinner last night, and most of us stare blankly into space like we just woke up from a medically induced coma.

3. Donuts are a quick fix, a moment of sweetness that fades just as quickly as it arrives. Many people go through life chasing donuts—temporary pleasures, quick successes, the next big thing—only to find themselves hungry again, searching for something more. But deep inside, we all wonder: Is there something that doesn't just fill us for a moment but sustains us forever?

—Stay Groovy

7

HALLOWEEN

File This Under: “What Was I Thinking?”

(Subtitle: *Because, as you’ll soon see, clearly, I wasn’t.*)

There comes a time in every young man’s life when he faces a pivotal, life-defining question:

Is fourteen too old to dress up as Scooby-Doo and fill a pillowcase with twenty-seven pounds of candy?

Answer: Oh, absolutely.

I learned this the hard way after last year’s ill-fated Halloween outing, when an elderly woman—who had clearly seen some things—gave me *that look.*

You know the one.

The look that said: *Aren’t you a little large to be a cartoon dog begging for sugar?*

So, I vowed. Never again.

New Year, New Plan.

This year, I wouldn’t be a dork in a dog suit.

I would be cool.

I would be rebellious.

I would...throw eggs at people.

(Note: Throwing eggs at people is neither cool nor recommended. Please refer to Exhibit A: My life that night.)

Now, I wasn't some hardened criminal. I wasn't even a wannabe thug.

Most of my "trouble" came from being profoundly immature rather than an actual menace to society. But that night? That night, I made some *poor life choices.*

The Truck of Doom

So there we were. Me. Dylan. Some other guy whose name was wiped from my memory by trauma. Just three underdogs, walking down the street, minding our own business. Until we heard trouble approaching.

It came in the form of a pickup truck carrying seven teenage jackals. Egged. Ready. Two in the cab. Five in the bed. Wild-eyed hooligans armed with eggs and zero regard for human dignity.

And they weren't just randomly throwing eggs.

No. These guys had standards. They chose their targets with military precision. And unfortunately—we looked ideal.

"INCOMING!"

The truck roared toward us. The egg bombardment began. These eggs weren't tossed—they were launched with full, unholy malice.

Fast.

Direct.

Like cruise missiles filled with cholesterol and pain.

How we dodged that storm of doom, I will never know. But somehow—miraculously—we escaped unscathed.

And then.

The Greatest Throw of My Life (Which Should Have Gotten Me Killed)

They sped away, cackling like hyenas, unaware of our miraculous escape.

Then, a thought occurred to me. A thought so reckless, so

profoundly dumb, that I now wonder if my teenage brain had the decision-making abilities of a baked potato.

I had an egg.

I had an arm of pure mediocrity.

And I had a once-in-a-lifetime opportunity.

So, I took it.

I lobbed that single egg into the night sky.

Picture this in slow motion: The egg soared up through the darkness—a beacon of justice.

The truck continued its escape, its passengers oblivious to the incoming retribution. And then—SPLAT.

A direct hit.

Yes, I, Bobby Niemond, had done this. The same Bobby Niemond who once hit my own Little League coach in the head during warmups and got benched before the game. I had just executed the most perfect egg strike in recorded history.

It was glorious.

It was poetic.

It was—

SHORT-LIVED.

Chaos Ensues

The taillights burn red as the truck *screeches* to a halt.

Immediate brake slam—sending two jackals immediately somersaulting over the hood. Landing on the pavement, only to slowly rise and then crumble again like dazed zombies.

And then—driver pulled off the most psychotic U-turn in history—which promptly launched two *more* jackals out of the truck bed. Same results. dazed zombies.

At this point, even the universe was against them.

Four jackals down.

One still barely clinging to the truck bed.

The truck sped in our direction.

Until, the driver slammed on the brakes *again,* sending the final jackal crashed down a few feet away from us. He staggered to his feet. Took two steps forward, then collapsed again in a heap of broken dreams.

It was beautiful.

It was terrifying.

And we still had two jackals left in the cab.

"THERE THEY ARE! GET 'EM!"

The silence was shattered by the driver's voice.

His sidekick looked at him like he was the dumbest person alive: "Dude. They are standing ten feet away, lit up by our own headlights."

But it didn't matter.

Because now—it was a foot race.

Two jackals.

Three underdogs.

And I made a tactical decision.

I yelled, "TO DYLAN'S HOUSE!"

Because, obviously, it's an international rule that once an underdog reaches home base, the bad guys must immediately stop pursuit.

Spoiler: Jackals do not care about international law.

No sooner had we collapsed on Dylan's plastic-covered couches, gasping for air, when...

THE JACKALS BURST THROUGH THE DOOR.

So much for the Geneva Convention.

They lunged.

We bolted.

Through the house.

Out the back door.

Across the sacred dichondra lawn (Sorry, Dylan's dad).

And then—

THE FENCE.

We launched ourselves over it.

Fueled entirely by adrenaline and regret.

Here's where home-field advantage kicked in.

Because we knew something they didn't: Rusty had been begging his dad for a pool.

And guess what? Rusty's dad finally delivered.

Two jackals.

Face-first.

Into the deep end.

And as we flipped back over the fence in victory, we heard two splashes.

Final Scoreboard: Underdogs 1, Jackals 0

Rusty's dad called the cops.

His German shepherd (who only understood commands in German) kept the jackals treading water.

~

Lessons Learned

1. Every now and then, life is fair. If only for twenty-seven seconds I, who once gave my Little League coach a lump on his head the size of a lemon with a warmup throw, had just pulled off the greatest egg strike in human history.

2. Most of the time, life is not fair. The Geneva Convention means nothing to teenage jackals. Even when it should, home base doesn't always equal safety.

3. Sometimes, lifesaving help comes from the most unexpected places. The real MVP? Rusty's dad and his long-overdue pool. Our last line of defense. The great escape. The only thing standing between us and being ripped apart by the Jackals. But what about the battles that aren't just games? Ever feel like life itself is relentless, exhausting, never letting up? Does anxiety chase you down, leaving you breathless? Does depression feel like a weight you can't shake? Where do you run when there's

nowhere left to hide? Is there a way to escape the jackals that live in your mind—the fear, the doubt, the exhaustion? And if real relief exists, where do you find it? What if the answer isn't where you expect, but in someone you've yet to trust?

— Stay Groovy

8

FAMOUS PEOPLE WHO LIVED IN PACIFIC PALISADES

Honorable Mention: Adam West.

Now, before you start yelling, "How dare you relegate Batman to an honorable mention?" let me explain.

Adam West—yes, the original Batman, the Caped Crusader of campy 1960s television glory—rightfully deserves a moment in the spotlight. However, since his legendary exploits have already been meticulously chronicled in a previous (historically accurate-ish) account, we will honor him here briefly, yet with the deepest reverence.

Because let's be real—Adam West was Batman, on-screen and off.

While other actors tried to escape their superhero personas, West doubled down. He didn't just live in the Palisades—he *patrolled* it, in spirit if not in full Bat regalia.

Did he have a Batcave? Unconfirmed but highly likely.

Were there tire tracks halfway up Palisades Drive leading to it? Rumors say yes.

Did he take strolls through the neighborhood humming his own theme song? We can only hope.

So while this is technically an honorable mention, make no

mistake: Adam West was, and forever will be, Batman of the Palisades. (Note proper use of *the*.)

Gilligan, the Local Oddity

When I say Gilligan lived in Pacific Palisades, let's be clear—I don't mean Bob Denver, the actor. Oh no.

I mean Gilligan, the full-time, shipwrecked persona who roamed the streets as if he had just rowed ashore from the S.S. Minnow.

It was *not uncommon* to see him wandering town in a sailor hat, bell-bottoms, and that unmistakable goofy smile, scanning the horizon like he was still searching for the crew.

"The Skipperrrr, the Millionaire and his wife, the Moo-ovie star, the Professor and Mary Ann… here on Gilligan's Ai—isle!"

(Wait. Did you just try to sing that?)

Now, if you spotted him at the grocery store—like he was about to build another radio out of coconuts—you had to wonder: *Isn't that… Bob Denver?*

No.

That was just Gilligan.

And he was fully leaning in.

Did he try to change his image? Nope.

Did he attempt to live a normal, post-Gilligan existence? Not a chance.

Did he ever think, *Hey, maybe it's time to retire the little white sailor hat?* Absolutely not.

In fact, rumor has it someone once tried to cast him in a serious drama, and the universe immediately rejected the idea.

The cameras wouldn't roll.

The lights refused to turn on.

The script pages spontaneously burst into flames.

Because Bob Denver was never meant to be Bob Denver again.

He was Gilligan—forever.

And the residents of Pacific Palisades had no choice but to accept it.

. . .

Mission: Unbearable

Yes, Peter Graves.

The *Mission: Impossible* Peter Graves.

The Hollywood legend.

The silver-haired icon.

The man whose very presence exuded sophistication, mystery, and the unmistakable air of knowing far too much about classified government secrets.

But none of that mattered.

Because at that moment, I was too busy experiencing my own social extinction.

The Scene of the Crime: Colvey's Men's Shop, a store so uncool no one had voluntarily entered it since the Eisenhower administration.

A museum of beige, brown, and deeply depressing shades of gray.

And yet, there we were. Shopping for cardigans.

Here I was, dressed in: corduroy bell-bottoms. A two-inch brown leather belt. Earth shoes—the ones that felt like they were designed for someone walking backward.

And my mother—the very woman who brought me into this world—decides that what I really need to complete this tragic ensemble is a sweater.

What was she thinking?

Didn't she realize I had sacrificed episodes of *Adam-12* and *Emergency!* for *this*?

Just when I thought my day couldn't get worse, the universe called in an airstrike of pure, unfiltered embarrassment.

Because Peter Graves walked in.

Now, you'd think a Hollywood icon casually browsing for knitwear might add a touch of class to this miserable errand.

Wrong.

Because in that moment, my mother—a fully grown adult with a mortgage and a driver's license—completely lost her mind.

She squealed.

She gasped.

She whispered, “It’s him! It’s him!” at a pitch so high that only dolphins could hear.

She went full fangirl.

And suddenly, I was the adult in this situation.

And I was not prepared.

Things I Considered Saying to Save My Dignity

“Mom, get a grip!” (*Risky.*)

“Woman, control yourself!” (*Very risky.*)

“Mom, this man makes a living by pretending!” (*Technically true, but we were way beyond that.*)

But I knew—deep in my soul—that saying anything would be as effective as trying to calm a mob of screaming teenage girls at the Santa Monica premiere of *HELP!*

My Final Descent Into Mortification

Colvey’s was silent.

You see, decorum was paramount when selecting sweaters.

This was the kind of reverent silence usually reserved for:

Museums.

Libraries.

I couldn’t scream. I couldn’t run. So I did the only thing I could. I stood there and turned several shades of embarrassment. Starting with the intense orange of an Arizona sunset and then shifting to the deep red of a Maine lobster.

I have no memory of how we left the store. Maybe I blackout-walked to the car. Maybe I astral projected out of sheer humiliation. All I know is that, for years, anytime the name Peter Graves was mentioned, my entire nervous system collapsed like a folding chair.

LIFE LESSONS from This Circus of Events

1. There's no expiration date on embarrassment. The moment you think you've aged out of public humiliation, life will personally intervene—it could be your own mother shrieking with joy over a half-priced sweater in a discount department store. If that fails, rest assured: your kids, spouse, or an ill-timed wardrobe malfunction will happily step in to seal your fate. (Pssst... check your zipper.)

2. Some people find their niche—and then refuse to leave it. Gilligan could have won an Oscar, but the universe said, Not gonna happen! Some people are so deeply committed to their brand that they become the brand—whether it's a castaway in a sailor hat, your uncle proudly rocking his high school letterman jacket (despite being eligible for AARP), or that outdated guy who signs off with "Stay Groovy."

3. Disguises only go so far. Adam West could stroll the Palisades in sunglasses, but everyone still knew he was Batman. But what about us? Can we truly hide behind a fresh start, a different city, or well-crafted excuses? Can shifting blame erase the past? Does justifying broken relationships make us innocent? Or heal what's been wounded? No matter how far we run, the real us always finds a way to surface. And when that moment comes—when we're left with nothing but who we truly are—what then? Will we be met with rejection? Judgment? Or is there someone who sees everything—the flaws, the failures, the regrets—and still whispers, "You are deeply loved. You are worthy"?

— Stay Groovy

9

THE MOST FAMOUS PERSON WHO LIVED IN PACIFIC PALISADES

Now, I know you're expecting me to drop a presidential name like former President Ronald Reagan.

Nah.

How about Eddie P? Next door neighbor who owned a Chevron gas station in town. But his real claim to fame? Are you sitting down for this?

Eddie was an extra on *Star Trek*. You know, one of those guys sprinting down the hallways of the USS Enterprise when it was under attack.

That would be NCC-1701 for you Trekkies.

Yeah, I know. When you live next to Hollywood royalty like this, you just learn to cope.

However, I always wondered why his wife would shush us because Eddie was "learning his lines."

"But, Mrs. P, Eddie doesn't have any lines."

Anyway, it's not him either.

The most famous people don't need introductions—but let's roll out the red carpet anyway.

It's none other than...

Wes Parker.

Dodger First Baseman.

1964-1972.

(Cue the stadium announcer in deep baritone: Now batting (echo), first base (echo), Wes (echo), Parker (echo)!)

Even today, when I see someone wearing number 28, I can't help but think, *You're wearing Wes Parker's uniform. Treat it with respect.*

Back When Baseball Was Baseball

Stirrups.

No batting gloves.

No designated hitters.

Back when men were men, the mound was high, and pitchers lasted eight innings and threw 150 pitches a game.

Can I get an amen?

Back when the phrase "Look for low and outside but watch for in your ear" was life-saving advice, not just a line from a movie.

The Routine: Scully at night, box score in the morning, Murray on Sundays.

Let's talk about Vin Scully. The gold standard of baseball announcers. The man was so good that people at Dodger Stadium brought transistor radios just to hear him call the game they were already watching live. Let that sink in.

You didn't need a TV because his descriptions painted the perfect picture:

Scully (or Vinny, as those of us in the know call him) was never in a hurry.

"Donatelli delivers, Wills reaches out and lifts a dying quail to right field that falls... in comes Lefebvre... in comes Parker... and the Dodgers lead... 2-1!"

And if Drysdale or Koufax was on the mound, that was all they needed.

You weren't sure if he was sitting in the room with you, telling a story, or calling a ball game in a press box miles away.

He'd start a story in the third inning and finish it somewhere in the seventh after a brief detour of the Kennedy administration and a fun fact about Belgian waffles.

It was Scully who once said of a well-turned 6-4-3 double play, "That was as smooth as Sinatra on a Saturday night."

The Farmer John commercials? They were just sizzling, savory interludes.

Mornings Were for Box Scores

Like a true scholar, my mornings were dedicated to a deep study of the box scores.

How did Parker do? Hits? How many and what kind? Single? Double? Triple?

What about the Three-Dog (Willie Davis) and Mota (pinch hitter extraordinaire)?

Errors? (I never had to worry about Parker's name appearing there —the dude was a vacuum cleaner in a baseball uniform.)

Was it a complete game? If not, who came in to relieve Singer? Perranoski?

And, of course, note the attendance. Because it wasn't just a number—it was a sacred figure bestowed upon us by the baseball gods.

Then there was Jim Murray of the *LA Times*—the Nobel laureate of sportswriters.

It was Murray who said, "Trying to hit Koufax was like trying to drink coffee with a fork.

And, "Koufax's curveball wasn't a pitch—it was a public execution."

Before anyone knew what happened, the umpire yelled, 'Strike Three!' Many a batter was befuddled, but it did not matter.

It was Murray who said about Scully: "Los Angeles didn't just get a baseball team in 1958. They got a voice. A voice that could tuck you into bed at night with the gentle hum of a transistor radio under your pillow. A voice that made your backyard feel like the front row at

Dodger Stadium. A voice that made heartbreak bearable and victory unforgettable.

"Vin Scully never needed a partner in the booth because, frankly, there wasn't enough room for two Rembrandts on one canvas.

Wes Parker and Me

We had a lot more in common than people think.

He hit for the cycle in New York. Yup, listened to it.

My full name? Robert *Wesley* Niemond.

See? *Way* more regal than Bobby, right?

I met Wes Parker twice:

1. Hughes Market—I bagged his groceries once as a box boy.

2. At a local country club, I almost ran him over with a golf cart rounding a corner.

Still counts. Because when it's your boyhood hero, it all counts.

Wes Parker: Defensive Genius

Let's talk defensive stats.

Fielding percentage: .996 out of 10,380 chances.

Six Gold Gloves.

Best first baseman not in the Hall of Fame.

And guess what? Neither am I!

Coincidence?

I think not.

We were both switch-hitters.

Him: Baseball.

Me: Wiffleball.

(But hey, the operative word here is *ball*.)

It's like we're identical twins—except he's thirteen years older and significantly better at baseball.

My dad's business season tickets meant I got to watch more Dodger/Padres and Dodger/Braves games than anyone should legally be forced to endure.

Back when the Padres were losing 100 games a season—and the

Braves not far behind—the Padres had the single greatest uniform challenge in history:

How do you make brown and yellow look cool?

Spoiler:

The Padres failed. Miserably. For fifty years.

They looked like they had lost a bet with a 1970s kitchen.

Of course, the Braves had one of the coolest uniforms—along with the St. Louis Cardinals.

But then they went through that weird pullover V-neck phase—you know, the one that screamed, "Disco isn't dead, and neither is my chest hair." (Never a good look—or phrase you want associated with a baseball uniform.)

Front Row Seat to Greatness

But those season tickets had one major perk.

Second row. First deck. Overlooking first base.

And unless The Hammer Hank Aaron was hitting, my eyes were locked on Wes Parker.

Even though he was just one deck below, I studied his every move with binoculars.

The silky-smooth footwork.

The way he tapped down the red Dodger Stadium clay to make sure no ball would get by him tonight.

The rare two-handed catch from a first baseman.

(Tried it. Harder than you think.)

It was as if he was moving in slow motion.

I'm pretty sure the song "Smooth Operator" was written about him.

And *that*, my friends, is why when anyone asks me who *the* most famous person who ever lived in the Palisades is, my answer will always be...

(said in a deep baritone announcer voice)

Wes (echo)

Parker (echo).

Were there lessons to be learned? By now, you know there were.

1. Uniforms matter! Oh, do they ever. Why did the 1984 Padres—decked out in mustard yellow, mud brown, and white shoes—fall to the Tigers and their timeless uniforms featuring the bold Old English "D"? Because the universe decreed it so. San Diego never had a chance.

2. *Heroes matter!* Having heroes or role models can be incredibly powerful. They provide inspiration, motivation, and a sense of direction. When we admire someone who excels in their field—whether it's an athlete, artist, scientist, or leader—it sets a standard for us to strive toward. Heroes remind us that success is possible with dedication and effort. They also shape our values, teaching us resilience, discipline, and passion.

3. *Mission matters.* From 1964 to 1972, Wes Parker embraced his calling as the Dodgers' first baseman, mastering his craft with dedication. For fifty years, Vin Scully brought baseball to life, his voice painting the game's drama with unmatched artistry. Jim Murray understood he was exactly where he needed to be, wielding the written word with brilliance. You might think, *But they had special talents that I don't possess.* And you'd be right—*sort of.* Not everyone is meant to play first base, call games, or craft poetic sports columns. But every one of us is capable of doing something that makes each of us feel, *this is why I'm here.* Here's the truth: anyone can excel at love. Starting tomorrow, make a conscious effort to love those around you—with intention, kindness, and patience. Especially those who are hardest to love. You'll be amazed at the results. In the end, you'll realize that loving others is your

true mission—a mission that never fades, never fails, and never ends. Because loving others fills more than it empties, unites more than it divides, and reflects the One who loved first. Embrace it and watch it transform your life—and the lives of those around you.

– Stay Groovy

10

MY BASEBALL CAREER

Lasted a nano-second

Required enormous self-discipline.

Centered around the number 3.

Let me explain.

A great high school player might have a three-hit game.

A good high school player might have a three-hit week. (We played two games a week in high school.)

But when's the last time you met someone who accomplished the rarest feat in baseball?

The three-hit career.

Yes, for my entire high school baseball career, I racked up exactly three hits.

One per year.

What Were My Three Legendary Hits?

Tenth grade: JV baseball. We were busy wondering why our jerseys had zippers and smelled like expired cheese. It happened, but I have no memory of it. This might be a metaphor for the entire season.

Eleventh grade: A weak single up the middle late in the game that broke up a no-hitter.

I remember this one because the first baseman looked ready to murder me when I arrived at first. Also because I hit the ball too close to my hands, and the feeling in all my fingers just returned last Tuesday.

Twelfth grade: My magnum opus. A pinch-hit double into the gap in right center. My best and most inconvenient hit. Inconvenient because I risked ruining my perfect streak.

By mid-eleventh grade, I realized if I played my cards right, I could achieve the impossible:

A three-hit career.

I had already achieved my "hit for the year" two years running. Now, all I had to do was get one next year and never risk another at-bat. The problem? I hit my double early in the season.

Now, I needed a strategy to keep Coach West from sending me back up to the plate.

Meet Coach West.

He was a really good football coach. But you had the feeling that he was the baseball coach because every coach was required to "coach" two sports. We were his "off" sport.

He had a short but predictable temper. You had the feeling that he woke up looking for a trash can to kick.

If you triggered him, you would hear, "CAN'T BELIEEEVE YOU [followed by your last name]!"

But he was predictable: Screw up and you'd earn the curse. Don't, and you didn't.

Once, in a rare moment of kindness, he gave me a game ball for how well I coached first base.

True story.

Either I was really good at waving runners, who hit obvious doubles, to second, or it was his way of saying, "Thanks for not playing today."

Since I had already gotten my "hit for the year," I needed to stay off Coach West's radar.

I mentally rehearsed my response in case he tried to send me up again.

Me: "Coach, statistically speaking, I have a perfect streak going, and I really think we should honor that historic achievement."

Coach W: *"CAN'T BELIEEEVE YOU, NIEMOND!"*

Thankfully, I never had to deliver my speech. So, he never delivered his.

Mission accomplished.

But wait—there's more.

The Plot Twist

Now, you might assume my three-hit varsity career meant I was bad at baseball.

And you'd be right about that.

But...

I also played American Legion ball, which picked up right after the high school season ended and ran through summer.

And in American Legion ball, I hit...(are you sitting down?)

THREE HOME RUNS!

That's right.

I turned a three-hit career into a three-dinger summer.

The same guy who barely managed one hit per season somehow launched three bombs.

Pretty sure this qualifies as the Eighth Wonder of the Baseball World—right behind the mystery of why I ever got a varsity jersey in the first place.

Let's break down the three legendary home runs because each is unique:

Home run #1: "The Shocker"

We played our home games at Jackie Robinson Stadium, UCLA's home field.

It was muggy. Evening game. Late innings. Maybe seven people in attendance.

I hit a ball down the left-field line and barely cleared the fence. I didn't even realize I hit a homer until I heard a teammate yell,

"NO WAY! NIEMOND JUST HIT A HOME RUN!"

That's how few people were there—I could hear individual reactions.

I don't remember running around the bases because I'd never done it before. However, the next day, as I walked onto campus, I heard a familiar voice. It was Coach West.

He ducked his head out the door and yelled, "HEY, BABE RUTH!" as I walked by.

I just sheepishly grinned.

Home run #2: "The Sweet Spot"

First at-bat of the game.

CRACK. Perfect contact.

I immediately took off, thinking, *This is definitely a single... maybe even a double.*

I slide into second like an absolute legend.

The shortstop looked at me and said in a tone of disgust, "What are you doing?"

Confused, I asked, "What do you mean?"

"The ball went over the fence, moron."

Embarrassed, I trotted around the bases.

Home run #3: "San Diego Debacle"

Tournament in San Diego.

No outfield fence. There were so many teams that not every game was played on fields with fences.

I smash a ball to deep right.

I take off sprinting.

I think: *I GOTTA STRETCH THIS INTO A TRIPLE!*

I reach third base and hear my teammates yelling: "HOME! HOME!"

Without hesitation, I book it for home.

Just before reaching the plate, I hear: "SLIDE! SLIDE!"

So I slide. Perfectly. Clean. Flawless.

Only then do I realize...

The right fielder gave up chasing it when it went over his head onto the asphalt basketball courts.

The ball was still rolling like a tumbleweed when I slid.

Pretty sure the shortstop from home run #2 was catching that day.

And the look of pure annoyance was way too familiar.

Meanwhile, our dugout was in tears, wheezing with laughter.

In Keeping with the Rule of Threes, Here Are Three Lessons From My Career in Baseball.

1. The three-hit career is more difficult than it seems. Anyone can get three hits in a game, but can you stretch them across three whole seasons? It takes discipline, patience, and an uncanny ability to avoid eye contact with your coach. Why be streaky when you can be perfectly, mathematically underwhelming? Some players dream of game-winning home runs. I mastered the art of statistical obscurity. And the game ball for not playing? Next-level strategy.

2. The home run trot is harder than it looks. It requires three key elements: Teammates who don't yell in stunned disbelief, "WAIT... THAT WENT OVER? Actually watching where the ball lands. Notice I was 0-3 on that critical point. Understanding that "home" and "slide" are not instructions for a ball still rolling 600 feet from home plate.

3. The answers we long for are closer than we think. If my identity had been tied to my baseball performance, wouldn't my three-hit career have crushed me? Wouldn't I have walked away believing I wasn't enough—because I hadn't done enough? This brings up the question: What happens when we fail? When our own expectations are not realized? When our mistakes cost more than we ever imagined? Does failure have the final word, or is there a way to face it without being defined by it? What if our worth was anchored to someone who never fails? If that were true, wouldn't failure lose its grip? Isn't that what we're all searching for? A place where regret doesn't define us, where forgiveness isn't earned but given? Where grace meets us when we least deserve it? And if it's out there—waiting for us—wouldn't that change everything?

— Stay Groovy

11

WATER FIGHTS: THE ONLY FORM OF WARFARE WHERE EVERYONE SURVIVES

Some battles in childhood were pure, harmless fun—where nobody really lost. Some, not so much.

Water fights? Absolutely.

Rock fights? Absolutely not.

Water fights were pure joy, an all-out battle of wills and water pressure where the only real injuries were soaked socks, and the emotional trauma of being hit with a bucket of water.

Rock fights, on the other hand, typically ended with someone clutching their forehead while both sides immediately entered into a crisis-level United Nations emergency summit to figure out how to tell someone's mom what just happened without getting all of us grounded for eternity.

And if there was one universal truth in childhood, it was this:

A mother in full-blown "YOU WERE THROWING WHAT AT EACH OTHER?" mode is more terrifying than the actual rock itself.

I have exactly one memory of a rock fight.

Because one mom, angry as molten lava, is all it takes.

One.

No more rock fights.

But water fights?

Oh, those were different.

Those were epic.

Those were legendary.

Those were high-stakes, Olympic-level splash battles where the only rule was get soaked or die trying. And two of them, in particular, deserve to be enshrined in history.

Battle 1: Bus vs. Bus—A Low-Speed Aquatic Showdown

This was no ordinary water fight.

This was a moving battlefield.

We're talking school buses.

Big, yellow, gas-guzzling land whales of education.

And on this fateful day, they became arenas of destruction.

The Setting:

The last days of junior high one year.

The temperature? Surface of the sun.

The students? Checked out.

The bus drivers? Also checked out.

The rules? Forgotten.

Enter Mr. C and Mr. Y.

Two bus drivers who had long abandoned the idea of controlling junior high kids and decided, *You know what? Let's just let them have at it..*

So, the stage was set.

Two buses.

Dozens of kids.

Weapons of mass saturation.

And one long stretch of Sunset Blvd. And then—

it happened.

The Plan:

We waited.

Quietly.

Patiently.

Like predators stalking their prey.

The moment both buses lined up, side by side on a straightaway?

IT. WAS. WAR.

Windows slid down.

Water balloons, and sheer reckless abandon were unleashed.

The Chaos:

Screams.

Shrieking laughter.

Meanwhile, the bus drivers had fully embraced their roles as charioteers of destruction.

It was glorious.

It was lawless.

It was middle-school mayhem at its peak.

And somehow, not a single adult intervened.

Because, let's be honest: the only rule during the last week of school is "If it keeps them entertained and nobody dies, let it happen."

And so it did.

Until one too many innocent bystanders (aka the nerds who mistakenly sat in the "dry zones") got soaked, and suddenly, complaints were filed.

By the time we got back to school, there were threats of "serious consequences."

But absolutely no one got punished.

Because even the teachers knew that a little low-speed aquatic warfare never hurt anybody.

Battle 2: The Apartment-Wide Water War of Sunset Blvd.

Now, my childhood wasn't exactly stable.

Thanks to multiple divorces and a general sense of "let's just see where life takes us" parenting, I lived in five different locations in the Palisades. Which means I don't just have childhood stories—I have a fully documented anthology of absolute mayhem from all over the Palisades.

This particular masterpiece of chaos took place at the apartments on Sunset, the ones where the street suddenly drops off into the abyss.

The layout? Important.

The alley behind the apartments? A full three stories including the parking garages.

The only windows? Unassuming bathroom sliders.

Why does this matter?

Oh, you'll see.

The Opening Salvo:

It started innocently enough.

A few kids.

A couple of cups of water.

Some lighthearted backyard ambushing.

I don't remember ever starting one, but joining in? Oh, absolutely.

But then—

the adults got involved.

More specifically, the dads.

Because let's be honest—moms have standards.

Moms are sacred beings who value things like clean floors, dry furniture, and raising children who don't engage in rock fights.

Dads?

Dads see a water fight and think, "Finally, my moment has come."

Because let's face it—men don't ever grow up.

They just get taller, gain access to better tools, and find new, more elaborate ways to cause chaos.

And when dads enter a water fight? It stops being a game and starts being an extreme sport.

Key Strategies Deployed by the Enemy (aka, Every Dad in the Building):

The High-Level Bombardment:

Someone realized that kids in water fights don't look up.

Buckets of water were dumped from those third-floor bathroom windows onto unsuspecting kids who thought they were being *stealthy*, slowly creeping around to ambush an adult.

I still remember the sequence:

The faint creak of a window you didn't even know could open. The tidal wave water cascading onto your unsuspecting head. The shock of realizing the ambush you planned had just ambushed *you*. The victorious, maniacal laughter of a dad who had just scored a direct hit.

Casualties: Extremely high.

The Window Ambush:

Walking past a closed window? Safe.

Walking past an open window? Surprise flash flood from a forty-year-old man who should have been paying bills.

The Hose of Doom:

Someone's dad had a garden hose.

And when a fully grown man with no remorse and unlimited water pressure enters the fight—

Game. Over.

The Aftermath:

The entire complex was drenched.

Kids were hiding under cars and in bushes.

At least one little brother was wrapped in a towel and carried inside like a fallen soldier.

And the dads? Laughing. Victorious. Zero guilt.

Final Scoreboard:

Rock Fight: Ended after one mom went Pompeii.

Bus Water Fight: Ended in vague administrative threats.

Apartment Water War: Ended with kids seeking shelter under bushes.

FINAL LESSONS from a Childhood of Hydrated Combat

1. Water warfare is the great equalizer. It doesn't matter if you're big, small, fast, or slow—everyone is fair game. Just ask the lady walking her dog on the sidewalk in front of the apartment that day.

2. Always look up. Because somewhere, someone is waiting —bucket in hand, giggling like a supervillain—ready to drench you. Maybe it's a prank, a rogue five-year-old, or a sibling settling a decade-old score. So always look up—in doorways, on balconies, and especially when trust feels suspiciously high.

3. Water fights end when Dad says they do. Because sometimes, all it takes is someone in authority to say, "We're done here," and it's over. The chaos stops. The fight ends. But what about the battles that don't end so easily? Not the ones with others—but the ones within. Ever wrestle with false guilt—the kind that whispers, *This is all my fault,* after a marriage falls apart? After life unravels. Ever feel the crushing weight of responsibility for things you were never meant to carry? What if there was someone with the authority to silence that voice? Someone not just powerful enough to rescue you but loving enough to walk with you through the pain, past the self-blame, and into something greater? Because sometimes, the thing we need rescuing from most is ourselves.

— Stay Groovy

12

THAT TIME I ACCIDENTALLY ORDERED 100 IMPERIAL STORMTROOPERS

Ever wake in the morning from a dream so intense that you sit up in bed, heart racing, and think, *What on earth was that?* A dream so strangely vivid that, unlike most fleeting visions, every detail lingers—etched into your mind as if it actually happened?

This is one of those dreams.

I dreamt I ordered a real Star Wars Imperial Stormtrooper—just one —as a conversation starter for social gatherings.

Instead, I apparently clicked one hundred.

So you can imagine, one unsuspecting morning, I found myself staring at my Ring doorbell notification in complete disbelief. The delivery guy stood there—behind him, an army of identical, white-armored, battle-ready troops.

When I opened the door, the delivery guy just shrugged and said, "You must have clicked one hundred in the dropdown." Then he left. Just like that. No takebacks. No exchanges. No chance to say, "Oops, my bad."

The trucks pulled away—yes, plural, because it took five to transport my accidental battalion.

As I stood there, my wife peered over my shoulder.

"Uh... what did you order?"

I, still processing, mumbled, "I thought... I ordered one."

She blinked at the perfectly aligned formation of plastic-clad warriors. "And they just... live here now?"

Apparently, yes. The moment I stepped aside, they marched inside in perfect unison, somehow all fitting in five flawless rows of twenty, our living room—which, might I remind you, is not that big. But hey, dream logic.

Situation 1: The Grocery Store Disaster

Life with Stormtroopers was *fine* until we ran out of coffee. My wife, seeing me struggle with the reality of one hundred fully armored roommates, handed me a grocery list and said, "You. Store. Now."

I figured I could handle this solo, but apparently, my Stormtroopers had other plans.

The officers (who, I should mention, were the only ones who spoke) insisted on accompanying me "for my protection." Because obviously, picking up almond milk at Trader Joe's is fraught with peril.

So there I was, pushing a cart down the aisle, a parade of armored troopers in single file behind me.

Shoppers froze. Employees whispered into radios.

A guy in a Chewbacca t-shirt rounded the corner and nearly passed out.

As I reached for a loaf of bread, the officer in charge barked in a radio-like voice, "OBJECT SECURED!"

At checkout, the cashier, wide-eyed, scanned my items. "Uh... do you need a bag?"

I turned to my commanding officer, who simply said, "WE REQUIRE NO BAGS."

I just tapped my card and left before Homeland Security got involved.

. . .

Situation 2: Stormtroopers vs. The HOA

It was only a matter of time before the Homeowners Association took notice.

Their first concern? "Um, sir, your guests are... in violation of permissible outside *decorations*."

I glanced outside. They were standing in perfect formation in the driveway. Just... *standing there.*

The HOA rep cleared his throat. "They've also been, uh... directing traffic?"

Apparently, when the school bus pulled up, the Stormtroopers took it upon themselves to block both ends of the street and usher children out in military-style precision.

One kid, obviously elated, shouted, "THE EMPIRE IS HERE!"

"Look," I said, "I didn't *ask* for this. They just... *exist* now."

The HOA guy, unimpressed, handed me a cease-and-desist order and walked off.

Situation 3: Date Night Disaster

For the sake of our sanity, my wife and I decided to go out for dinner. Alone.

Or so we thought.

We arrived at our table, ordered wine, and for about five peaceful minutes, things were normal.

Then, the waiter froze mid-step.

I turned.

Three Stormtroopers stood at attention by the entrance.

I sighed and waved them off. They left.

Thirty seconds later, four more appeared.

"We are... NOT DOING THIS," my wife sternly warned.

I got up and shooed them outside, where I found the entire battalion stationed around the perimeter of the restaurant.

A man at the next table whispered, "Honey, I think something *very illegal* is happening."

We finished dinner quickly.

. . .

Situation 4: The Birthday Party Debacle

Somehow, word got out.

And by "word," I mean all neighborhood kids realized that I was apparently in possession of a small imperial army.

Which is how I ended up accidentally hosting my neighbor's kid's Star Wars-themed birthday party.

I walked outside that afternoon to find a crowd of children in Jedi costumes, wielding plastic lightsabers, ready for battle.

Their parents? Sitting on lawn chairs, sipping coffee, assuming I had planned this.

A little boy in a Yoda hat pointed a blue lightsaber at me and shouted, "WE CHALLENGE YOUR STORMTROOPERS!"

The officer in charge nodded solemnly.

I barely had time to shout "NO, NO, NO" before the Stormtroopers charged, and a full-scale galactic battle broke out in my front yard.

It lasted three hours.

At one point, a Stormtrooper toppled in dramatic slow motion, much to the glee of a particularly determined seven-year-old, and rolled into our flower bed.

That's when my wife pulled me aside and said, "Fix this!"

I placed an emergency pizza order and handed out Capri Suns like a battlefield medic, bringing an end to the world's most momentous Jedi vs. Stormtrooper conflict to keep the kids from overthrowing the entire Empire.

The neighborhood kids stormed off like a conquering army, their foam lightsabers held high, whooping and hollering with the unrestrained chaos of warriors fresh from battle. Together, they roared their anthem, "BEST. PARTY. EVER!"

Meanwhile, the Troopers limped back inside—their plastic armor dinged and scuffed, dignity shattered, and morale at an all-time low, utterly defeated by a horde of Capri-fueled children half their size. The commanding officer simply shook his head and whispered, "This will *not* be recorded in Imperial archives."

The HOA left furious, delivering me yet another citation.

LESSONS? Always! Even in dreams.

1. Details are important. Always double-check the Dropdown Menu. A simple click can change your whole life. Maybe it's an accidental purchase. Maybe it's booking a flight to Paris, France, which takes you to Paris, Texas. Either way, attention to detail matters.

2. HOAs are powerful. They can and will take down the Empire. You may think Darth Vader was powerful. But he's got nothing on an HOA president with a clipboard.

3. The battle is real. I woke from my dream exhausted, as if I had truly spent the night commanding an army of inept Stormtroopers. But as I sat up, still groggy, one thought remained—some battles aren't just dreams. Do you ever feel like life is a battle? A quiet but unrelenting fight for your well-being, a war for hope, a daily struggle to find purpose and meaning? Do you ever feel like, no matter how much effort you give, you're slowly losing ground? Have you ever wondered, Is there anyone who can pull me out of this? Is there someone who can rescue me from this ever-deepening sense of emptiness? Could there be someone—someone whose life IS recorded in an ancient archive—who has already overcome the very struggles that threaten to consume you? Not just offering a fleeting escape, but something real, something lasting?

— Stay Groovy

13

SEMINARY: THE UNEXPECTED JOURNEY IN JEANS

When you hear the word *seminary*, what comes to mind?

If your imagination summons young men in long black robes speed-walking across an Ivy League-looking campus—solemn, silent, and celibate—you're not alone. That's the picture many carry.

But let me offer a different snapshot: picture a guy in jeans, juggling theology textbooks, marriage, and a second cup of coffee. Welcome to my world.

I attended Talbot School of Theology in La Mirada, California. I'm married. I talk more than I should—especially if silence lasts longer than three minutes. And yes, I once handed in a paper dressed in a gorilla suit. You'll see.

The Reluctant Seminarian

To be honest, seminary wasn't on my bucket list. Not even close. UCLA had already taken a few years off my life, thanks to a tug-of-war between social distractions, hard science classes (thank you, Organic Chemistry), and not-yet-knowing-Jesus. Spoiler alert: The world should be thankful I didn't become a doctor.

So, how did I end up signing up for four more years of school? I had just become a follower of Jesus and wanted to know more about the Bible. I even tried bargaining my way into Bible college instead. But the academic advisor, seeing my twenty-five-year-old self with an undergrad already in hand, wisely nudged me forward: "Seminary isn't essential. But it's efficient. It'll save you ten years of trying to learn this on your own."

And then came the kicker: the 3.0 GPA requirement. You actually had to be *good* at school—B average is good. I'd never seen a consistent B in my life. C was my companion, my steady old friend. I'm pretty I would have been voted "Most Likely to Be Average" in high school.

Thankfully, I wasn't alone. I had a few brothers-in-arms—like Bill, who carpooled with me for four years and practically carried me across the graduation stage. And Mark, who saved me from Hermeneutics before I even knew what a commentary was.

Let me walk you through three classes that shaped my life. And yes—every story here is 100 percent true. (It kind of has to be.)

Class 1: Hermeneutics (Her-ma-nu-tics... yeah, me neither)

This was the class where you learn to interpret Scripture—how to read the Bible *without* turning it into a choose-your-own-adventure book.

The professor was brilliant. So were the students. So brilliant, in fact, I couldn't even *understand* their questions, let alone the answers. We were told to write a paper on a "problem passage." I thought, *Perfect. That's all of them.*

Then he added, "Don't pick something easy like 'Who was Melchizedek?'"

Naturally, I stayed after class and asked, "So... who was that Mel guy again?"

He smiled. "You can do your paper on him."

Things didn't improve from there. I didn't even know what a

commentary was. Thank God for Mark, who walked me to the library section where the smart people live.

Then came the due date. Papers were due *before* class. No exceptions. None. Five minutes late, and it was a zero. The only excuse was a death certificate. Your own.

The night before, a tech-savvy undergrad offered to print my paper. I noticed a gorilla suit hanging in his closet. So when the printer failed and class had already started, I did what any desperate future theologian would do: I suited up, sprinted into class mid-lecture, stuffed my paper into the stack, and sprinted back out. At the break, I returned—gorilla-free—and took my seat.

The professor looked up and said, "Glad you could join us, Mr. Niemond," as the room burst into laughter.

Turns out I wasn't as anonymous as I thought. I was the only one missing before the break. But hey—no penalty. The professor must have appreciated the commitment.

Class 2: Greek (aka, Daily Humble Pie)

If you want to read the New Testament in its original language, you have to wrestle with Greek.

Our class started at 7:30 a.m. That meant leaving my West LA home in the dark to reach La Mirada by sunrise.

Every morning began with a quiz: four words from a list of twenty-five. Not in your seat when the bell rings, and you could not take the quiz. Miss one? You're down to a B. Miss two? Welcome to average. Miss all four? Time to reconsider your calling.

And then there was Mason. Always late. Every day he flew into the parking lot at 7:29, flung open his car door, hurdled a bush or two, and crash-landed into his seat right as the bell rang.

Every. Single. Class.

If there were a grade for athleticism, Mason would've have aced the class.

. . .

Class 3: Theology

These were the game-changers. Theology I, II, and III. We covered everything: the Bible, God, Jesus, the Holy Spirit, sin, salvation, angels, the Church, end times... the whole story. Almost four decades later, I still have my notes.

But what stuck with me most wasn't just the content—it was the character of the professors. These weren't just scholars. They were shepherds. Gentle, thoughtful men who lived what they taught. I learned as much from *who they were* as from *what they said.*

Final Thoughts

Talbot is named after Louis Talbot. He passed by the time I started, but during registration, his widow handed me a copy of his biography. The title? *For This I Was Born.*

Which brings us to our final three reflections:

1. Do you know why you were born? Not just your job or your profession, but your deeper purpose; the reason for your existence? The Bible says, "It's in Christ that we find out who we are and what we are living for" (Ephesians 1:11, MSG). Following Jesus reveals our identity and calling in a way nothing else can.

2. It was Louis Talbot who said, "Preach to broken hearts." Is your heart broken? Are you tired, discouraged, disillusioned, or carrying guilt or grief? Psalm 34:18 tells us, "The Lord is close to the brokenhearted; he rescues those whose spirits are crushed" (NLT) If your heart is hurting—whether from unmet expectations, painful losses, or wounds from others—Jesus invites you to come to Him, just as you are.

3. Heaven isn't full of good people—it's full of forgiven people. What everyone in heaven has in common is not perfection, but forgiveness through Jesus. Tell him what hurts. Ask Him to forgive you. You'll be amazed by what happens. I was—and I still am. As Psalm 62:8 says, "Pour out your heart to God" (NLT).

— Stay Groovy

14

BOY SCOUTS

I was a proud member of Troop 400, back when being a Boy Scout was the coolest thing you could do that didn't involve a dirt bike or a slingshot. Troops 223 and 90 were the other big dogs in our area, if memory serves. I'm pretty sure we had better uniforms and flashier Dutch oven recipes.

Scouting back then was a serious affair. We had a strong tradition—weekly meetings, monthly campouts, summer camps, and Court of Honor ceremonies, where scouts were awarded their Eagle badges.

Every week, we'd gather as an entire troop. It was the first time I operated in a formal system of ranks: Tenderfoot, Second Class, First Class, Star, Life, and finally Eagle.

Each scout belonged to a patrol. Mine? The Lone Pine Patrol. The name was perfect—noble, resilient. I still remember some of my comrades: Kenny, who could start a fire with a potato chip, and Alex, who could not start a fire even with a blowtorch and divine intervention.

Every month, we'd pack up our gear, hop in our parents' cars, and head to the Southern California mountains. These weren't glamorcamping trips with RVs and Wi-Fi. No, these were the "dig your own latrine" kind of trips. Real deal. Rustic. And fun.

Every campout featured the inevitable newbie Tenderfoot wandering into your campsite asking one of the classics:

"Can you help me find a bacon stretcher?"

"Do you have a left-handed smoke shifter?"

We'd send him toward the next camp. Always away from where he came. Because it didn't exist. It was Scout hazing at its finest, and a rite of passage—like being swarmed by ants because you stored your trail mix in your sleeping bag.

We were required to cook our meals—start the fire with flint and ignite cotton balls *not* soaked in anything flammable (which was an inspection issue). But the milk chilled in the stream and the unmistakable crunch of Captain Crunch at breakfast told a different story about our rustic purity.

We spent full weeks at Camp Wolverton in Sequoia and Emerald Bay on Catalina Island. Emerald Bay was a surreal experience. First of all, I woke up to Reveillé for the first time. Have you ever been violently summoned from sleep by a trumpet? It's like being chased awake by a brass-wielding banshee.

And then came the infamous rattlesnake hike. Our patrol went out one night for a hike. Half of us had passed a certain spot on the trail when we heard it: *the rattle*. You know the one. The one that says, "If you move, you might become an unwilling science lesson."

The snake was angry and in a cactus clump right next to the trail. No room to go around. So, naturally, we came up with the most scout-like, rational solution: Everyone sprints past it at the same time and hopes for the best.

I've never run so fast. I probably hit a personal best in the forty-yard dash. My boots didn't even touch the ground.

Then there was the mile swim, a requirement for the swimming merit badge. But it wasn't a "gentle loop around the pool" mile. Oh no. It was at dawn, in the glacial waters off Catalina Island. Mind you, this was when I had the body fat of a carrot. You haven't truly questioned your life choices until you've tried to swim through a hypothermic panic attack.

. . .

Row Boats, Order of the Arrow, and Philmont.

To earn the rowing merit badge, we had to maneuver red rowboats around pristine white yacht hulls. Think about that for a second. Red paint. White fiberglass. Boy Scouts. What could possibly go wrong?

Now, rowing comes with one small design flaw: you're supposed to row forward while facing backward. Which meant we were essentially steering a 200-pound bathtub blindfolded through a floating Ferrari dealership. The harbormaster should've just rung a dinner bell and shouted, "Gentlemen, start your collisions."

The results were... artistic. Oar blades scraped along hulls like calligraphy pens. Rowboat bows kissed yachts with all the tenderness of a shopping cart hitting a Lexus. By the end, the marina looked like Picasso had switched from oils to Krylon spray paint. Bold, red streaks everywhere. Abstract expressionism, brought to you by the Boy Scouts of America.

Then came the Order of the Arrow—the elite club of scouting. The "tap-out" ceremony was legendary: over 300 scouts standing in a massive circle around a bonfire that could probably be seen from Mars. Staff in Native American garb dancing and whooping like warriors selecting their champions, grabbing the shoulders of those chosen for this secret brotherhood.

Once tapped, we were told to take a vow of silence. I know what you're thinking. No, I did not become the first scout eliminated at the tap-out ceremony. This was serious stuff. We're talking "if you groan when you're hungry, you're out" silence.

We were told to grab our sleeping bags, then led—alone—to a remote part of the island where we'd sleep with nothing but our thoughts and—you guessed it—rattlesnakes.

The next day, we were told we'd be rewarded with French toast for breakfast, only to find out it was one slice. Total. For everyone. It was a carb-based test of character.

People ask what we did during the day at Order of the Arrow.

Nothing out of the ordinary—just some light dock-cleaning... with our toothbrushes. Because apparently, character is built one bristle at a time.

One moment lives in infamy: The Pajama Fiasco.

In my frantic dash to grab my sleeping bag after being tapped out, my pajamas—flannel, plaid, and unfortunately very visible—slipped out and landed smack in the middle of the main camp. I didn't notice, but everyone else did.

When the vow of silence lifted, so did any pretense of dignity. Retrieval required me to walk into the center of camp and reclaim them—like Arthur pulling the sword from the stone, only more awkward and with fewer cheers. Let's just say humility was no longer an abstract concept.

PHILMONT: The crown jewel of Boy Scout life.

Philmont Scout Ranch in New Mexico. A high-adventure trek, only open to the higher ranks, that promised lifelong bonding—and delivered matching foot blisters. It's where we earned our 50-Miler badge, which, in case you're wondering, involves actually hiking 50 miles in boots made of questionable leather and teenage optimism.

And as if that weren't enough adventure, our adult leaders were *MIA* the first few days due to—you guessed it—high blood pressure. So it was just us teens, a greenhorn from the staff, a stack of topographical maps no one knew how to fold, and a collective fear of bears so intense we hung everything—everything-in trees, including one guy's socks just to be safe.

We survived on trail mix, freeze-dried regret, and the sheer willpower of Randy, who swore he saw Sasquatch but kept hiking anyway.

Looking back, Scouting wasn't just merit badges, mosquito bites, or half-cooked chili. It was a proving ground. A laboratory of leadership, laughter, and life lessons. It taught me how to tie knots, start fires, and—more importantly—how to persevere through rattlesnakes, rogue pajamas, and one slice of French toast.

And yes, somewhere along the trail—probably somewhere near a cactus—I became an Eagle Scout.

LESSONS? Always.

1. Rattlesnakes don't wait for permission. Sometimes you've just got to run. Plans are great, maps are helpful, but when you hear that angry rattle two feet off the trail in the dark of night, it's time to run. Life rarely gives a five-minute warning before things get real, which is why agility, prayer, and decent ankle support go a long way.

2. Always pack extra pajamas... and your dignity. When it comes to explaining to 300 scouts why SpongeBob was your sleepwear of choice, you've learned an important lesson: humility comes standard in the great outdoors. Embarrassment builds character and is temporary. Campfire stories are forever. And yes, dignity is recoverable. Eventually.

3. Be prepared... for something greater. We were told to be ready for the weather, the wilderness, and the occasional bear. But life demands deeper readiness: for heartbreak, change, and unexpected detours. The Scout motto, "Be prepared," points to more than gear—it whispers of grace. The One who made the mountains walks beside us in the valleys. So when the trail gets rough, be prepared—not just with supplies, but with the quiet confidence that you're not alone. Be prepared to ask for help and forgiveness because we all need both.

— Stay Groovy

15

VAIL: PART 1

The year was 1980. I had just graduated from UCLA, armed with a degree and no earthly clue what to do with it. While other friends donned ties and tried out terms like *synergy* and *ROI*, I slipped on snow boots and moved to Vail, Colorado, for one ski season. Just a temporary layover between youth and, well... whatever it is people do when they stop ordering off the kids' menu of life.

My dad, ever the practical man, had a backup plan. He told me he knew a guy in Dallas who could get me a job in banking. Banking. Can you picture me in banking? Me neither. I thought checks and balances had to do with Eastern European gymnastics. The only balance I was interested in was the one required to get off a ski lift without taking out a family from Des Moines.

So off to Vail I went—my first time living out of state, my first time in the Rockies, and my first time realizing that air could hurt your face. I arrived early, before the real cold kicked in. Skies were still blue. The air smelled of pine and hope. Then winter slammed in like it had something to prove.

Early memories stick:

I played tennis at high altitude once. Just once. The balls didn't bounce—they *ascended*. I wasn't playing tennis. I was participating in a low-orbit experiment for NASA.

I skied on K2 610s with Look turntable bindings and Lange boots so stiff, they made walking to the chairlift feel like military training. But I was ready. I had dreams. I had youth.

I learned quickly that surviving winter in a ski town required more than warm socks and optimism. It demanded secrets known only to the locals and the wise:

- Carry a cigarette lighter, not for smoking. No, this was to heat the key to *thaw your car locks*. Yes, kids, there was a time before fobs and apps. Back then, we fought frost with fire and courage.
- Flip your wipers at night. Because nothing says "bad morning" like realizing your windshield wipers are now frozen abstract art.
- Carmex. It was a statement. It said, "I live in Vail, and I like having lips."
- Sorels. The boots of champions. I wore mine until the soles surrendered and walked off without me.
- Driving in first gear. It wasn't just a driving speed—it was a local secret weapon. Chains were for tourists.
- Keep a down sleeping bag in your car. Because if you got stranded—and you would—you didn't want your obituary to say, "Died stylishly cold in his VW van."
- Credit cards. Useful for scraping ice, scraping frost, and scraping the bottom of your bank account. Occasionally, they bought food too.

To pay the rent (and maybe delay real life a little longer), I picked up odd jobs:

I waited tables at a fancy-schmancy restaurant where "captains" roamed the dining floor like royalty. My job? Do the work. Their job?

Take the tips. It was my first and last time waiting in a restaurant that featured captains. Mr. Fussy Pants, our captain, never quite understood that people didn't come to Vail for foie gras—they came to ski. Colorado may be called "Little Texas," but trust me, nobody in boots wanted bananas flambé.

Then I landed a "prestigious" role at a candy shop. Still in business today, by the way (you're welcome, economy). According to my American Express application, I was *vice president of foreign sales.* Technically true. There were two of us. And I was the one who stocked the German chocolate. That counts, right? It was international commerce with nougat.

But the crown jewel of employment? Dishwasher.

Yes, mindless dishwashing. It paid the rent, didn't require customer service, and left plenty of time for introspection. I washed, I thought, I skied. I had my own rhythm.

And in my spare time, I got *productive.*

I even picked up a teaching diploma from the prestigious Aspen State Teachers College. Totally fake, but it *looked* amazing. I mailed it home and waited for reactions. My mom framed it. That woman could find a mother's pride in a paper hat.

Which brings me to my next role:

I was Santa Claus for the town of Vail.

Not metaphorically. Literally. I *was* Santa Claus. The town needed one. I had a fondness for making people smile. Done deal. They gave me a suit and two instructions:

1. Spread Christmas cheer.
2. Show up to light the giant tree on Friday night at seven sharp.

I took the first task seriously. I skied in full Santa gear. I directed traffic as Santa. I barged into a live radio show and did a surprise interview as Santa. We discussed sleigh technology, reindeer unions, and the secrets of chimney navigation. The DJ gave "Santa sightings" all week: "I hear Santa is skiing under Chair Eleven, kids..."

It was magical.

Until it got... weird.

Everywhere I went, people whispered, "The Secret Service was just in here asking about you." At the ski shop. At the chocolate shop. The restaurant.

Naturally, I thought it was a joke. I mean, how hard could I be to find? I was literally parading around in red velvet with bells on. Was I accidentally evading the federal government? Was *I* a national security threat? Had someone ratted out my fake diploma?

Turns out, both former President Gerald Ford and Vice President Walter Mondale were scheduled to appear *onstage* with Santa Claus at the tree lighting. That Santa being... me.

Fast forward to Friday night, here I was, backstage, heart pounding, beard slightly askew, while a crowd of hundreds chanted, "SANTA! SANTA! SANTA!" waiting for me to magically light the tree.

Meanwhile, the Secret Service agents were all in a panic, speaking frantically into their wrist radios: "We hear the crowd, but we haven't vetted him yet..." (I'm not making this up)

Vetted me? I *was* Santa. Shouldn't that come with automatic clearance?

Eventually, they let me through. I don't know if it was Christmas magic, fear of a riot, or the sheer absurdity of the situation. I climbed those stairs with the full weight of America's childhood dreams on my shoulders—and a dozen machine guns pointed at my back from under unzipped ski parkas.

I didn't flinch.

Okay, I *slightly* flinched.

And yes, the thought did cross my mind—to bonk their heads together like Moe from *The Three Stooges*. Just a quick "nyuk-nyuk" to break the tension. Would it have been unforgettable? Sure. But also, almost certainly, my final act as a living human. I had a strong sense the Secret Service didn't share my appreciation for physical comedy.

Plus, I didn't want the headlines to read: "Santa Claus Neutralized in Vail—Reindeer at Large."

So I did the only thing left to do. I smiled, ho-ho-hoed with authority, and lit that tree like the fate of Christmas—and possibly my pulse—depended on it.

And in that moment, something strange and wonderful happened. I felt it: awe, joy, and yes, the distinct sensation that one wrong move might get me tackled by an agent named Doug wearing mirrored sunglasses, at night, who has no sense of irony.

It was fun.

It was absurd.

It was Vail.

HERE'S what I took away from my ridiculous, snow-covered detour in Vail:

1. Some stories are so unbelievable, they need proof. So if you're one of those skeptical types who thinks I'm making up the part about Santa, the Secret Service, and nearly getting flash-tackled on a snowy stage—don't worry, I'm not offended. Click here. (And if the link's broken, just know that the truth is out there... probably hiding behind a beard and a reindeer.)

2. When you're not sure what to do with your life, it's okay to take a break and ski. Just don't turn it into a decades-long spiritual sabbatical in a lift line. Skiing in your early twenties is soul-searching. Skiing through your fifties while waiting for a sign is... snow denial. At some point, hang up the poles and ask some deeper questions.

3. And finally, it would've been easy to miss what was quietly unfolding beneath the snow and silliness: a spiritual journey. It started subtly—between the thinking afforded by dishwashing shifts, powder runs and pretending to be

Santa—but something deeper was stirring. I didn't have the words for it then. Now I do. Read Part 2. It's where the real light started to break through the snow.

— Stay Groovy

16

VAIL: PART 2

Vail wasn't just a scenic detour in my life—it became an unexpected spiritual trailhead.

I didn't know exactly what I was looking for back then. I only knew I hadn't found it yet. And somehow, I trusted I'd know when I did. Dating felt like an emotional carnival ride—exhilarating at first, but always ending with a dizzying, painful letdown. So, no, "it" wasn't there. Partying offered even less: a fast pass to hangovers and regret, punctuated by shame-filled stories others loved to retell. Still, I was searching. For what? I couldn't say.

There was one night etched in my memory like a bruise you keep pressing on. I took Tina, a cowgirl from Texas, to see a movie. I was careful to frame it as a casual, friendly outing. No pressure. Just two friends seeing a movie. *Ordinary People*, it was called. What an ironic title. For someone raised in the shadow of emotional landmines and family dysfunction, that movie wasn't "ordinary." It was a direct hit.

Somewhere between the credits and the parking lot, something inside me ruptured. I tried to hold it together, but as soon as we got in the car, I crumbled. The tears came hard and fast—years of grief and confusion breaking the surface. I choked out, "I think I just need to take you home."

I was a mess—undone, embarrassed, raw.

Tina didn't flinch because she knew. She seemed to understand something I couldn't yet name. Later, she and others would help me see what I was too guarded to admit: I was an orphaned soul. Lonely. Searching. Longing for something, someone, who made sense.

All I knew at the time was this: avoid movies with the words *Ordinary* or *People* in the title.

A few weeks later came what I now call my "E.F. Hutton" moment. Remember those commercials? The whole restaurant would fall silent when someone said, "My broker is E.F. Hutton... and E.F. Hutton says..."

It happened at a church potluck, of all places. I was at a buffet table when someone across the room called out, "Hey Bob, I didn't know you were a Christian!" Without thinking, I shouted back, "Oh yeah, I'm a Christian now."

The room froze. Forks hovered mid-air. Everyone stared. So I added, "Or not."

Awkward silence.

Turns out Christianity involved more than scoring free food in a church basement. Who knew?

Still, even with my half-baked theology and spiritual clumsiness, God was drawing me in quietly, patiently. Even when I couldn't see it.

Not long after, Tina invited me to a Christian concert. A what? I didn't know Christians *did* concerts. I thought they sang hymns in pews and left the concerts to the Doobie Brothers.

I hesitated. Then I made a deal.

"Can we sit in the back row?"

"Yes."

"On the aisle?"

"Yep."

"Can I leave if I need to?"

"Absolutely."

So I went. The place was packed—standing room only—and yet, somehow, it felt like I was the only one there. I couldn't leave if I wanted to. I was glued to my seat. The speaker's voice cut through the noise inside me. The message was simple: "Some of you are sitting on the fence. It's time to make a decision."

I walked out of that concert shaken. Not converted but confronted. I didn't know what that decision would look like—or when I'd make it—but I knew the fence was no longer an option.

The next part of my journey came through two powerful realities: irresistible love and irrefutable truth. In that order. God had them waiting for me in an unlikely place—a tiny church just outside of town.

Growing up, church felt like background noise during my parents' multiple divorces. It was irrelevant at best, painful at worst. So as soon as I could opt out, I did. Not even Christmas or Easter pulled me back in.

So walking into church again—after almost a decade away—felt more foreign than familiar. I was skeptical and guarded.

The day I visited, there were only a few cars in the snowy lot. Not a great sign. Just one set of footprints leading inside. Worse sign. I cracked the door open, hoping to peek in quietly, when the pastor looked up and said, "Great, here's someone! Now we can begin."

Wait—*me?* He was waiting on *me*?

I couldn't back out now.

I walked in and sat in the third row. It was me, the pastor, his wife, and eventually a handful of others. I don't remember much of the sermons. What I do remember was this: every week, after church, the twelve or so folks there would move the pulpit, set up tables and chairs, and eat together.

Want to know how you spell irresistible love for a broke, searching ski bum? F-R-E-E F-O-O-D.

But it wasn't just the meals. It was the welcome. The warmth. These people didn't just tolerate me—they honored me. And for the life of me, I could not understand why.

Who *were* these people?

They weren't just feeding me lunch. They were feeding something deeper—something hollow inside me.

And then God introduced irrefutable truth.

Her name was Sallie.

At first, Sallie was a regular at church. Then I heard her name during a Sunday prayer request. She was extremely ill, so allergic to nearly everything that she had to live in a near-sterile environment. But when I visited her, expecting frailty, I found something else entirely.

Her body may have been breaking down, but her spirit radiated strength. Her faith had muscle. I asked questions—*a lot* of questions. Not to debate, but to understand.

Years later she told me she could barely finish one answer before I was ready with another "But what about" question.

"But what about evolution?"

"But what about pain?"

"But what about hypocrisy in the church?"

She was my walking version of www.gotquestions.org —decades before it existed.

Sallie didn't rush me. She listened, smiled, and answered patiently. She helped me replace my awkward "Christian—or not" answer at the church potluck with real understanding. A faith I could stand on, not just wonder about.

Sallie never married and went home to Jesus in 2021. But her fingerprints are still on my faith. She helped build the scaffolding that holds me up to this day. And yes, years later, I had the opportunity to visit with her and thank her in person.

Vail was more than a mountain town. It was sacred ground. A place where free food, late-night tears, potlucks, unlikely friendships, and small-town churches cracked open my heart just wide enough for God to step in.

And He did. Gently. Decisively. Permanently.

Takeaways?

. . .

1. Orphans long to belong. The tears I shed in the car after watching Ordinary People weren't just about the film—they were the unfiltered cry of a soul that had wandered too long without a home. I couldn't name the ache back then, but now I know: I was an orphaned soul. Not in the legal sense, but in the spiritual one—disconnected, uncertain, and aching for the deep, anchoring love of a Father. For a place, a person, a Presence, where I could finally say, "I belong." And I'm not alone.

Many of us carry a quiet ache beneath our grown-up exterior. We wear adult skin and carry adult responsibilities, but buried beneath the surface is a tender, unspoken question: *Am I truly seen? Would anyone stay if I unraveled?* We keep the ache at bay with noise, success, distraction—but it never fully disappears.

Jesus spoke directly to that ache. To grown men—men with calloused hands from years of fishing, self-made minds shaped by survival, and hearts more accustomed to silence than to sentiment. And yet to them, He said, "I will not leave you as orphans." (John 14:18). He wasn't speaking to children. He was naming something buried deep inside men who had never been taught to admit such longing.

That promise wasn't just for them. It's for us. The orphaned parts of our hearts—the ones still searching for love, for security, for home—are not forgotten. They are pursued. Found. Claimed.

2. Look for God in unexpected places. He doesn't always show up with thunder or lightning. Sometimes, He's hiding in a potluck. Or a snowy parking lot. Or at a Christian concert. At the time, I wasn't chasing God so much as stumbling through the fog of my own questions. And yet, He kept leaving breadcrumbs—through awkward church moments, free meals, quiet kindness, and an unshakable inner pull. If someone had told me Vail would be where my heart would soften toward faith, I would've laughed. But that's the thing about God: He often moves in subtle, sacred ways. Don't discount the common. That's often where the divine sneaks in.

. . .

3. Everyone needs a Sallie. Sallie was not famous. She never published a book or spoke to thousands. But she showed up. She made space for my questions—not with prepackaged answers, but with patience, truth, and love. I brought doubts, and she brought grace. I brought chaos, and she offered clarity. She was weak in body, but strong in spirit—proof that God often uses the seemingly fragile to do His strongest work. We all need a Sallie—someone who listens well, loves deeply, and isn't afraid to tell us the truth. And maybe, someday, we'll become that person for someone else.

— Stay Groovy

17

THE 4TH OF JULY RACE – PALISADES STYLE

BY SOMEONE WHO'S CLEARLY NEVER RECOVERED AND MAY STILL BE WANDERING THE COURSE

Think Norman Rockwell with better tans, and you've got a pretty good picture of growing up in Pacific Palisades. In some ways, it was magical—like living in a postcard.

But no day bottled that hometown magic like the Fourth of July. I'm not saying other towns don't try, bless their little patriotic hearts, but unless your day starts with a race, throws in a parade, and ends with fireworks, you're just lighting a sparkler and calling it freedom.

The race? Officially called the Palisades Will Rogers 5K & 10K Run. Unofficially, it's called "That Thing You Do Once and Then Lie About Forever." The 5K was added probably after someone watched me race and thought, "He looks like a solid halfway-er."

Now, let's settle something important. The winner of this race should be awarded the Greifinger Award. Why? Because every time I saw someone running, it was a Greifinger. I don't know how many of them there are. I suspect cloning. I once saw three pass me before I hit the first water station. All smiling. None sweating. Possibly robots.

Sure, other people have won the race multiple times. That's adorable. They can write their own story. This one's mine. And in this universe, Greifinger wins. Always. That's how alternate timelines work. Ask Marvel.

. . .

MILE 0—THE Regret Registration Moment

It began as all terrible ideas do, with way too much confidence and not nearly enough adult supervision. I was on my laptop, caffeinated and cocky, scrolling through Fourth of July events when I saw it: "Palisades Will Rogers 10K – Register Now!"

And my brain, which clearly hates me, whispered: *You've got this.*

I clicked *Register* like I was signing up for a beach picnic, not a public mental breakdown. The form asked for my T-shirt size. I selected Medium because hope is a delusion, and I hadn't seen a salad since Cinco de Mayo.

Then came the fateful dropdown:

5K or 10K?

And I, fueled by patriotism and self-deception, chose 10K like I had just been recruited for a Nike commercial. I ignored the little voice in my head whispering, *You cried during spin class last week...*

A few clicks later, it was done. I was in. I received a confirmation email titled:

Congratulations!

Which is code for:

We'll see you sobbing near the eucalyptus at Mile 4.

I started prepping like it was the Olympic Trials. I bought new running shoes from a place called *Red, White, and Wheezing*. I did one training jog around the block, immediately pulled something in my soul, and decided to carbo-load aggressively... for the next three weeks.

By race day, I hadn't run more than two miles without stopping for a cinnamon roll and a nap, but I showed up anyway. Because I was brave. And stupid. Mostly stupid.

Welcome to Mile 0.

The only mile powered entirely by lies, peer pressure, and a tragic misunderstanding of my current fitness level. I hadn't run a step yet, and I was already sore.

. . .

MILE 1—THE False Hope Festival

I started strong, waving to the crowd. The theme from *Rocky* was blaring. My legs felt powerful, and I briefly entertained the thought: *Maybe I'm a natural-born runner.* (Plot twist: I'm not.) I hadn't even reached the incline yet. The first mile was downhill. I let adrenaline, ego, and someone's dog named Baxter pace me to a personal record. This was a terrible mistake.

MILE 2—THE Water Station of Existential Crisis

I knew I was in trouble when a mom pushing twins in a stroller passed me while sipping iced coffee. I reached the water station like it was an oasis in a desert. A teenager handed me a paper cup with the enthusiasm of someone being forced to volunteer by their mom to earn back phone privileges. I missed my mouth. Half the cup went up my nose. I also considered starting a podcast about how running is a scam. I was seriously wondering if dropping out was un-American.

MILE 3—THE Disintegration Derby

Everything hurt, and nothing was okay. My left knee was plotting a rebellion. A man dressed as Abraham Lincoln power-walked past me, eating a banana. I wanted to cry, but I was too dehydrated. I seriously contemplated faking a hamstring injury and asking a stranger for a piggyback. I would have sold a kidney for a popsicle. I continued toward despair and chafing. I started calculating whether quitting would be considered treason.

MILE 4—THE Will Rogers Wipeout

I'm now ascending the switchbacks through Will Rogers Park. I can smell eucalyptus, regret, and one guy's overambitious use of body spray. I try to smile at the volunteers, but my face is stuck in "decomposing possum" mode. A child offers me encouragement. I hiss back.

. . .

Mile 5—The Phantom Cramp Parade

My legs are cramping in places I didn't know had muscles. I tried to stretch mid-run and took out a group of nuns like a bowling ball. A man in jorts yells, "Almost there!" and I vow to track him down after the race and report him to someone. I am dragging my left leg like a horror movie extra.

Mile 6.2—The Finish Line Fiasco

My quads are cooked, my dignity is gone, and someone dressed as George Washington passes me—while texting. I started seeing mirages—water fountains, medals, and forgiveness. I sprinted the last 100 yards looking like a drunk ostrich in a wind tunnel. I crossed the finish line with all the grace of a walrus falling out of a hammock. In my head, I heard the *Chariots of Fire* theme. In reality, I sounded like an old vacuum cleaner giving up.

Post-Race Cool Down

After the race, I collapsed on the grass like a Wi-Fi router during a Zoom call—blinking, overheating, and totally useless My legs were twitching, and I was fairly certain my thighs were now the consistency of rotisserie chicken—crispy on the outside, sobbing on the inside.

A volunteer handed me a medal the size of a coaster and said, "Great job!"

I asked, "For what? Not dying?"

Someone offered me a banana. I stared at it like it was a tax form.

A woman in glittery shorts casually asked if I was ready to sign up for next year. I laughed so hard I pulled something.

For the rest of the day, I waddled around like a penguin in bowling shoes. Every step was a negotiation, and stairs were a hate crime.

I was like a giraffe learning to salsa. All knees, no rhythm, and a high probability of tipping over.

Moms clutched their children as I wobbled by—like I was a tipsy clown on a unicycle juggling fire.

I wore my race shirt proudly, not because I earned it, but because it hurt too much to lift my arms to change clothes.

And as I soaked my feet in a bucket of ice and regret, I thought: *That was the dumbest thing I've ever done. I'm definitely doing it again next year.*

~

THREE LESSONS I Learned From the Race

1. Some things sound better in your head. Like "10K on the 4th of July." Or "I bet I can keep pace with that nineteen-year-old in compression socks." Spoiler alert: I could not.

2. Chafing is real, and it has no respect for your dreams. You can hydrate, stretch, and wear the right shoes—but one rogue seam, and suddenly you're walking like a cowboy in a spaghetti western.

3. Grace doesn't reward the perfect run—it carries the believing heart to a finish line it could never reach alone. Here's the thing about grace: it helps you do what you were never meant to do alone—finish the race. And I don't just mean the final breath we all take someday. Everyone dies. The real finish line is dying with someone who gives you what the world can't offer—assurance. The deep, unshakable peace that, when it's all over, you won't be alone. You won't be lost in some cold, cosmic, endless silence. You'll be home. In the presence of your Creator. Your Redeemer. Your King. Forever. Who wouldn't want that?

— Stay Groovy

18

MARRIAGE: PART 1

This year, my wife and I will celebrate twenty-nine years of happy marriage. (*Applause.*) Thank you. Thank you.

We'll also be celebrating our fortieth wedding anniversary.

Now, I'm not saying I've got it all figured out—clearly the math shows I haven't—but I *did* discover something amazing. I call it the Rosetta Stone of Marriage. Just like the original cracked ancient Egyptian hieroglyphs, this list cracks a far more cryptic code: the ten mysterious words wives use to describe literally anything.

This is historic. You'll remember where you were when you first read it—like when man walked on the moon, or when your wife said, "That's fine," and you didn't realize she meant your funeral.

Men, memorize these. Tattoo them somewhere private. Share them at sleepovers. Whisper them to each other over brisket.

So here it is. Ten phrases—each one seemingly harmless, like a kitten in a teacup, but loaded with marital consequence. Learn these, and you might just survive. Or even thrive. Ignore them, and you're one forgotten anniversary away from sleeping next to the dog. And not the cute one. The one that farts.

. . .

TERM #1: *Thing*

Simple, but deadly.

"Honey, I need more of those red things."

Do NOT ask questions. Do NOT say "What things?" Just nod. Smile. And pray. If you're a seasoned husband, you'll know she means that one oddly specific item that lives in a shoebox behind four suitcases and the ghost of Christmas Past.

Correct response: "Of course. How many?"

Wrong response: "Define 'thing.'" (Congratulations, you're now a "single thing.")

TERM #2: *Thingy*

This is a social grenade wrapped in casual phrasing.

"What was that thingy your cousin mentioned?"

Here's the thing: you don't remember. She doesn't either. But you're expected to. So what do you do?

Correct response: "Lemme call him right now."

Bonus move: Actually call. Use the word *thingy*. Your cousin will know if he's married.

TERM #3: *Thing-a-ma-jig*

Garage-related. Definitely loud. Occasionally sparks. Always followed by, "Wait... was that supposed to happen?"

"Can you use the thing-a-ma-jig to cut that wood?"

Do *not* say "Do you mean the circular saw?" or the even more suicidal "Wouldn't it be easier to say, 'power tool'?" That's how good men end up on missing person posters in post offices.

Correct response: "Absolutely." (Then go to the garage and pretend you're moments away from solving a mystery only men understand.)

TERM #4: *Whatchamacallit*

Non-food. Possibly decorative. Absolutely critical.

"Can you pick up the whatchamacallit on your way home?"

You will *not* know what it is. That's the point. This is marriage dodgeball. Ask the wrong question, and you're emotionally concussed.

Correct response: "What aisle is that on again?" If she says 'barbecue stuff,' it's code for charcoal briquettes.

Wrong response: "How in the name of Costco am I supposed to know what that is?"

TERM #5: *Doohickey*

Usually a car part. Possibly imaginary.

"The doohickey's broken again."

This could refer to the seatbelt, glove box, radio, or transmission. Or the vibe. Who knows.

Correct response: Pop the hood. Doesn't matter if the problem is inside the car—popping the hood buys you *Google Time*.

TERM #6: *Gizmo*

Electronic. Glowing. Vanished.

"Where's the gizmo?"

If you hold up the wrong thing (like the remote), prepare for impact.

Correct response: Hold up all devices you own, like you're being mugged by technology.

Pro tip: If she says, "Yes, that's it," hand it over and immediately order another one on Amazon before she changes her mind and says it's *your* gizmo.

TERM #7: *Whatsit*

Danger level: HIGH

"I loved that last whatsit you bought."

This is likely a melon. Or a lotion. Or a candle that smells like autumn and regret.

Correct response: Go to the store. Walk to the produce aisle. Find a married male employee. Say, "Whatsit." He'll nod solemnly and take you to the cantaloupes.

Important note: Female employees will sneer and walk away. Single male employees will panic and hide in the back room.

TERM #8: *Doodad*

Translation: Something technical. Wi-Fi? Plumbing? Thermostat? Ghost portal? Who knows.

Used in a sentence: "Can you fix the doodad?"

Best bet: Reboot the router, adjust the thermostat, wiggle a pipe, and act exhausted.

Bonus points for saying, "Looks like the flux capacitor's on the fritz again."

TERM #9: *Gadget*

Battery-powered, potentially marital-ending.

"Have you seen the gadget?"

Correct response: "I think I saw it Thursday." (Always Thursday. It's the Switzerland of vague timelines.)

Marriage veterans know: Any reference to "last Thursday" buys time, peace, and possibly forgiveness.

TERM #10: *Whatsitcalled*

"Can we go to that whatsitcalled?"

This is a test. It's always a test. And somehow, it's *your* job to know what "whatsitcalled" means—even if she just made it up. You're expected to be fluent in mind-reading and Yelp reviews.

Correct response: "Absolutely. The one with the patio, right?" (Patios are safe guesses.)

Wrong response: "The what?" That's not just a wrong answer—it's an emotional booby trap. You might as well say, "I haven't listened to a word you've said since Tuesday."

BONUS TERM: *Stuff*

"Can you bring me my stuff?"

This is not a question. It's a spiritual obstacle course. And you, brave soul, have been chosen.

Correct response: Grab four random things and yell, "I brought options!"

Chances are one of them is close enough to count. Bonus points if it's soft and smells like lavender.

Wrong response: "What stuff?"

Congratulations. You've just failed the relationship equivalent of a pop quiz in a class you didn't know you were taking.

She'll stare at you like you forgot your vows, your anniversary, and her dog's middle name—all at once.

Pro tip: If she's not pointing to it, it could be *anything.*

A purse, a scarf, a charger, a leftover sandwich.

Once, it was a memory foam neck pillow from 2006.

Even the angels were confused.

Stuff. You don't find it. It finds you.

And you better hope you're worthy.

MARRIAGE SURVIVAL HOTLINE: 912

Confused? Lost in a "thingy" time warp? Just dial 912—it's like 911 but staffed by battle-hardened husbands who survived the Great Thing-a-ma-gic Disaster of 2013. They're all married. All wounded. But somehow... still alive.

And if you've already blown it? Call 911. Tell them to bring chocolate. And a blanket. You're gonna need it.

. . .

A Loving Plea to the Ladies

While your husband is heroically trying to memorize the Ten Sacred Things—like he's prepping for a pop quiz in Klingon —may I offer a humble, heartfelt request?

Please, for the sake of peace, puppies, and the sanctity of our remaining brain cells, stop using two mystery terms in the same sentence.

"Honey, where's the whatchamacallit your friend mentioned at the thing last month?"

Do you see what just happened there? That's vague squared.

That's a Category 5 Confusion Storm.

That's how good men end up talking with the cat at 3 a.m.

And while we're at it, could you please bring us up to date on the conversations you've been having with yourself over the past six months?

Because when you suddenly ask: "What did she mean when she said that thing about him while they were at the whatsitcalled?"

We don't know.

We weren't there.

We're not even sure you were.

We're just standing in the kitchen holding a sponge like it's a lie detector test.

So we ask, respectfully:

- Please don't begin a sentence with pronouns. "She said it was there" is not a sentence—it's a riddle wrapped in a mystery wrapped in a throw pillow.
- If you change the name of something, send a memo. "Thingy" was the blender yesterday. Today it's the cat's medication. We can't keep up.
- If it happened in a dream, please don't hold it against us. We weren't there. Technically, neither were you.

THREE LESSONS...

1. Communication is everything—especially when you realize "thing" could mean forty-seven different objects and one unresolved argument. Learn to decode, clarify gently, and never, ever say, "Be more specific" unless you enjoy sleeping diagonally on the couch.

2. Laughter is essential. If you can't laugh at yourself (or the fact that you just bought the wrong "thingy" for the third time), you're missing out on one of marriage's best survival tools.

3. Love covers a multitude of missed cues. You won't always get it right—there will be misreads, wrong "thingies," and moments you both stare at each other like you're speaking different languages. But grace fills the gaps. Patience keeps the rhythm. And forgiveness keeps the light on. Take it from the One who invented marriage: love never fails. And even when ours does, His doesn't.

– Stay Groovy

19

MARRIAGE: PART 2

Disclaimer: what you're about to read contains exaggerated moments, misplaced confidence, emotional misfires, and one very sincere husband who graduated *summa cum laude* from the University of Missing the Point.

This is not marriage advice. This is written by a man who once duct-taped a sponge to a power drill and called it "efficiency."

If you're here for wisdom, lower your expectations.

If you're here to laugh, you're in the right place.

Now buckle up, keep your hands and feelings inside the ride at all times, and maybe grab a cookie.

TEN TIMES I Tried to Fix My Wife's Comments with Duct Tape... and How That Turned Out (Like You Didn't Already Know)

1. *"We need to communicate better."*

Fix: Duct-taped two walkie-talkies to our pillows. Called it "Pillow Talk 2.0."

Result: Accidentally tuned into a trucker named Big Randy.

He now gives me marriage tips.

They're... not bad, actually.

2. *"You never listen to me."*

Fix: Taped my ears wide open like a human satellite dish.

Result: She laughed hysterically. I couldn't blink. The dog threw up.

She finally stopped laughing long enough to say, "I don't need your ears *open*. I need your heart *on*."

Then she kissed my cheek and gently removed the tape.

Along with half my eyebrows.

Love hurts.

3. *"You don't help with the baby."*

Fix: Duct-taped the baby monitor to my chest like I was going on a Navy SEAL mission... to the nursery.

Result: At 3 a.m., "Baby Shark" blasted through my ribcage at full volume.

I shot out of bed, roundhouse kicked a lamp and saluted a diaper.

She was already up, feeding the baby—unimpressed and whispering, "Stand down, Captain Chaos."

4. *"I need you to be more transparent."*

Fix: Showed up to dinner wearing nothing but a clear rain poncho. Nothing underneath. Carried duct tape as a fashion accessory.

Result: Three neighbors called the HOA, one called their therapist, and the dog won't make eye contact.

We don't talk about that night.

5. *"You're emotionally distant."*

FIX: Taped a photo of us to my chest and said, "See? I Care."

Result: I sweat through the tape, and the photo slid off mid-conversation.

Metaphors. Everywhere.

6. *"We never go on real dates anymore."*

FIX: Duct-taped two lawn chairs to the truck bed, grabbed Taco Bell, and parked under the stars. Branded it "The Deluxe Date Night."

Result: A raccoon approached, locked eyes with me, sniffed the air, and slowly backed away—shaking his head.

Even *he* knew romance had left the building.

She smiled, and said, "This is ridiculous... and weirdly kind of perfect. Next time, maybe fewer varmints. But you? You're still my favorite disaster."

7. *"You're always glued to your phone."*

FIX: Duct-taped my phone to the ceiling so I couldn't touch it. Declared, "Behold! I am fully present!"

Result: Got a crick in my neck, twenty-three unread texts from her—including one that said, *You know I'm in the room, right?*

Then she sat next to me, handed me popcorn, and whispered, "Next time, just hold my hand. No ceiling mounts required."

8. *"Our curtains are outdated."*

FIX: Duct-taped a flannel bed sheet to the window frame. Called it "Rustic Mountain Cabin Aesthetic."

Result: It sagged in the middle, smelled like college, and blocked exactly zero sunlight.

She walked in, stared for a moment, and said, "This feels less like interior design... and more like we're hiding from the law. Next time, let's try *drapes*... not drama."

9. *"Sometimes I just want to be held."*

FIX: Wrapped us both in duct tape like a two-person survival burrito.

Result: We tipped over a chair, stuck to the rug, and had to Google "how to peel duct tape off a loved one without ruining the relationship."

She laughed so hard she snorted, leaned into me, and said, "This is wildly unnecessary...but also kind of adorable. Next time, less tape. More arms."

10. *"The dog keeps peeing on the carpet."*

FIX: Duct-taped a ShamWow to his belly and called it "Auto-absorb mode."

Result: He peed, panicked, and ran laps—leaving a wet crop circle on the rug.

Now the carpet's ruined, the dog has trust issues, and I'm listed in his memoir as "The Man Who Snapped."

MAN-TO-MAN ADVICE

Look—we get it. Words like *emotionally available* and *vulnerable* sound less like character strengths and more like things you caught from sitting too close to a scented candle.

"Doc, I think I have Vulnerable. I cried during a Folgers commercial."

So here's the deal:

You don't have to fix anything.

You don't have to say the perfect thing.

You just have to stay in the room and care.

Nod. Listen. Blink occasionally.

And when you're ready, reach for her hand.

Because as scary as it feels to show up with your heart instead of your hardware.

She's not looking for a repairman.

She's looking for *you.*

Baby steps, champ.

You've got this.

Also—maybe skip the poncho this time.

Three Takeaways

1. You can't duct tape your way out of a conversation. You can try, but she'll just peel it off—and then the conversation's longer and louder. Bonus: now you're bald in one spot.

2. Duct tape fixes hoses, bumpers, and probably three of your childhood injuries. But it does not fix trust, vulnerability, or the look she gives you when you say, "What did I do?" instead of, "I'm here for you." You want a better marriage? Put the tape down. Pick her up.

3. Real love isn't about fixing everything—it's about being present. Sometimes the best thing you can do isn't to solve the problem—it's to sit in the mess with her, quietly, willingly, patiently. That's the kind of love that doesn't break, doesn't peel, and doesn't need tape to hold. The

kind that reflects Someone who didn't fix us from afar—but stepped in, got close, and stayed. Because duct tape can't fix the cracks only grace can reach. For that, you don't need tape—you need a Savior.

— Stay Groovy

20

TRADER JOE'S: PART 1

Dear Sirs:

I write to you today not as a bitter person—but as a slightly sticky, sleep-deprived, emotionally combustible crusader of grocery justice. If I had friends, they would've staged an intervention by now. There'd be candles. There'd be snacks. There'd be a well-meaning PowerPoint titled: "Zapplewick: Sit Down and Log Off."

But alas. There are no friends.

There is only me...

And a half-empty jar of cookie butter that's been ignoring my texts since Wednesday.

I lit a candle. I played Norah Jones. I whispered, "We used to be something," like a character in a French film—too many scarves, not enough closure.

And yet, it just sat there—judging me with its smug, creamy, almondy silence.

Emotionally withholding. Spiritually aggressive.

Probably a Scorpio.

So now here I am:

Alone. Unsupervised. Unshowered.

Typing this with fingers sticky from both snack residue and betrayal.

Fueled by three cold brew samplers and the kind of angst usually reserved for printer jams and group texts without context.

And now—*now*—I present my Ten Greatest Grievances™.

Not in any particular order.

And absolutely not as a homework assignment from my psychiatrist.

Okay, maybe it is. Still counts.

It's a list.

A righteous list.

Let the record show:

You poked the bear.

And now the bear writes letters.

1. Parking

I once drove down *four* aisles looking for a parking spot. FOUR.

That's not shopping—that's a *pilgrimage*.

By aisle two, I was making deals with the universe.

By aisle three, I was speaking fluent dolphin.

By aisle four, I was legally feral and crying.

Here's my extremely reasonable solution:

Assign shopping days based on the first letter of your last name.

That way, upstanding Z-name citizens like me—Zapplewick, PhD in Patience and Parking Lot Warfare—aren't left circling the asphalt like sad vultures with social anxiety.

And NO, this has nothing—*NOTHING*—to do with "Z" being statistically rare and thus granting me 100 percent front-row access every time.

This is democracy in action.

Justice. Math. Divine will.

Pick one.

Totally fair.

Totally rational.

Totally screamed into my steering wheel until the horn gave up and just started sobbing with me.

2. Key Lime Pie

You discontinued it. WITHOUT WARNING.

No email. No whisper from the frozen aisle oracle.

Not even a psychic nose-tingle.

One day it was there—glowing like the sun.

The next? Gone.

Like trust. Like hope.

Like every relationship I tried to start after 2013.

I had to go to rehab. *Real* rehab.

They took my shoelaces, my dignity, and my commemorative Key Lime Pie tote bag.

I shared a room with a man named Todd who wept openly every time someone mentioned limes, citrus, or Florida.

On day three he whispered, "They never even let me say goodbye."

We hugged.

We healed.

Kind of.

My one allotted phone?

I used it to call Trader Joe's.

The manager—who I can only describe as a smug tiki in a Hawaiian shirt—informed me, with zero remorse: "It's a seasonal item. We only stock it when key limes are available."

LIES.

Key limes are not endangered alpacas.

They are not hand-harvested during a solar eclipse by monks in silk aprons.

They are fruit.

They grow year-round—in warm climates and broken hearts.

The rehab bill?

Out-of-pocket.

My HMO denied it under "grocer-related despair."

I tried to appeal.

The claims adjuster offered me a fig bar and whispered, "They did it to me too."

I have since started a Key Lime Pie Survivors Support Group.

We meet every Wednesday in a church basement.

There are folding chairs, strong coffee, and an emotional support parrot named Winston.

We take turns reading old product descriptions from the Trader Joe's website.

Sometimes we cry.

Sometimes we bake questionable substitutes and try to convince each other it's "just as good."

It isn't.

If you care at all—and I mean even one ounce—you will bring it back.

Don't make me storm the freezer aisle in my robe again.

I still have a court date pending from the last time.

3. Root Beer Float Popsicles

These should be classified as controlled substances.

I blacked out after my third box and woke up behind the store, clutching a half-melted wrapper, a popsicle stick in my pocket, and a stranger whispering, "You got any more of those icy boys?"

I didn't know who he was, but I trusted him.

We made eye contact. We understood each other. We were survivors.

I had sugar in my hair and stickiness in places I'm still too emotionally raw to discuss.

A raccoon tried to barter with me for a box.

He offered me an Apple Watch and what might've been a human tooth.

I almost said yes.

These aren't snacks—they're weapons-grade nostalgia.

They're creamy, root-beer flavored portals back to the one summer I felt truly alive, and my uncle still talked to me.

There should be a federal limit: one box per person per week.

Unless you've developed "alternate procurement strategies," such as paying off teenagers in the parking lot.

(Not saying I did this. Just saying I'm Venmo friends with Tyler, seventeen, who once wore a fake mustache and called himself "Uncle Carl" to get me an extra box.)

I now refer to my freezer as The Vault and guard it like I'm running a black-market dessert cartel.

If you ever pull these from shelves again, I will fully disintegrate into a cold, creamy puddle of regret.

And I will take Tyler down with me.

4. Cashier Inquiries

"Did you find what you were looking for?"

Honestly?

I walked in looking for eggs and left spiraling into a full-blown existential crisis.

What was I looking for?

Meaning? Purpose?

Someone who wouldn't ghost me after one date and a homemade lasagna so rich it legally qualifies as a cry for help?

I stood in front of the cheese display for seventeen minutes, hoping brie could answer questions my therapist couldn't.

Spoiler: It could not.

It just melted slightly and judged me.

And yes, this is the part where I once again apologize for the "incident" that led to the manager calling the police.

But in my defense, when I screamed, *"WHAT AISLE IS EMOTIONAL STABILITY IN?"* I wasn't yelling *at* anyone.

I was yelling *with* my inner child.

To the cashier named Becky: I'm truly sorry.

For the tears.

The confetti. (Long story.)

And the moment I curled up in the produce section whispering, "It's never just about the avocados."

I was two seconds from launching a podcast right there in aisle five.

Title: *Grapes of Wrath and Unprocessed Emotions.*

But also... maybe warn people before asking life-altering questions at checkout.

Just hand me my cauliflower rice and let me unravel in peace.

5. The "Do You Have Plans Today?" Trap

Do I—*do I have plans*?

Wow. Okay. Sure.

Let me just open the emotional floodgates while I swipe my reusable bag full of self-doubt.

Yes, I have plans. BIG plans.

I'm going to the DMV to renew a license I let expire because time isn't real anymore.

Then I'm heading to Petco, where I'll try to lock eyes with a lizard named Phil and ask, "Do you believe in love after loss?"

And then—strap in—I'm going to therapy, where my counselor will ask, "How have you been sleeping?"

And I will sob into a couch pillow and whisper: "Trader Joe's discontinued the root beer cream popsicles."

Again.

So if you're actually interested in coming along, fantastic.

Buckle up. Bring snacks. Wear comfortable shoes.

This journey includes at least two parking meltdowns and a spontaneous existential crisis in the frozen aisle.

(Spoiler: It's triggered by the cauliflower gnocchi I keep buying and pretending I like.)

Also: BYO tissues, water bottle, and emotional helmet.

We're not just running errands—we're processing trauma.

Sorry for yelling.

Again.

But seriously—don't ask questions you're not ready to hear the answers to.

Especially when I'm armed with feelings and two tote bags full of unresolved issues.

~

LESSONS? Always.

1. The parking lot is basically the Hunger Games—but with Kombucha. If you've never prayed in tongues, try circling a Trader Joe's lot for the fourth time while a Subaru Outback pretends it's leaving, only to "just check one more thing inside." That moment you scream into your steering wheel, and it cries back? Sanctification. Or psychotic break. Could go either way.

2. Root Beer Float Popsicles will ruin your life, and you'll say thank you. These frozen time machines are so emotionally potent they should come with a chaperone, a liability waiver, and a recovery hotline that begins with: "Hi, we've been there."

3. Sometimes the question isn't "Did you find what you were looking for?"—it's "What are you looking for... really?" And that's when the gospel sneaks in—right there in the cheese aisle. When you realize that no key lime pie, no perfectly ripe avocado, no perky cashier named Becky can fill the God-shaped hole in your soul. You didn't just come for snacks. You came hoping someone, somewhere, would see you. And friend—someone does. Even in aisle four. He's looking for you.

— Stay Groovy

21

TRADER JOE'S: PART 2

And now back to the list:

6. The Bells

The bell system. Oh yes. The sacred clang of doom that governs your store like a bizarre game of retail Morse code.

Let me see if I have this right:

One ring: Someone can't find the almond butter.

Two rings: A customer just asked, "What's umami?" and no one knows.

Three rings: Activate DEFCON Trader Joe's. Someone in a Costco hoodie is emotionally unstable and hoarding frozen gnocchi.

Last week, I heard the bell go off like it was possessed. The manager was slamming it nonstop while yelling "SECURITY!" and describing "a distressed individual wearing a Costco ensemble, mumbling about seasonal cheese."

Yes.

That was me.

In my defense, it was laundry day and emotional resilience is not my strong suit.

Also, shoutout to the customer who reached into his tote bag, pulled out a cucumber like it was a tactical baton, and asked, "Is there a problem here?"

Yes.

There was.

It's me. Hi. I'm the problem; it's me.

And I probably should not have tried to *sing it* in the middle of that chaos, but in my defense, it *was catchy* and I *was spiraling*. I think I made eye contact with a thirteen-year-old who was singing it with me.

For the record, I didn't mean to escalate things. I just panicked. The bell does that to me now. I've developed a full-blown Pavlovian response. Anytime I hear a ding, I drop to the floor and whisper, "I just wanted coconut shrimp and peace."

Please consider reworking your bell system to something less triggering—like smoke signals. Or trained ferrets. Anything but the bells.

7. Chicken Tikka Masala

Okay.

This isn't funny anymore.

I heard a *rumor*—and by rumor, I mean a whispered panic attack between two yoga moms near the cauliflower gnocchi—that you might be discontinuing the Chicken Tikka Masala.

I'm sorry.

EXCUSE ME?

That's not just a product. That's a life raft. A reason to get out of bed. A warm, saucy hug for the soul.

You don't just "maybe" discontinue that. That's like NASA saying, "We're thinking of phasing out oxygen."

Let's get one thing clear:

Chickens are not seasonal.

They do not migrate. They do not take sabbaticals. They are not part-time employees of nature.

They are available year-round—just like my unresolved emotional issues.

If you even *think* about removing this dish, I swear on every unopened bottle of curry simmer sauce in my pantry, I will:

Sing a mournful ballad, "Curry on my Wayward Son," while sobbing into a naan wrapper.

And when the police arrive—and they *will*—I'll look them straight in the eye and say, "I plead hungry."

So please. For the love of all that's spicy and sacred, leave it alone.

Because if you take away the Chicken Tikka Masala, you're not just breaking hearts.

You're committing a freezer aisle felony.

8. Samples

Do not hand me a single, cube of cheese on a wheat cracker and expect me to walk away emotionally fulfilled. I didn't come here for a sample. I came here for closure.

I need a bite that heals my inner child, that whispers, *You were always enough, even when your mom packed you off-brand pudding.*

A bite that repairs my marriage, rekindles my sense of wonder, and undoes the time I screamed, "WHERE IS THE LOVE?!" at a cashier named Greg while standing next to the free coffee station.

What you gave me was a quarter-inch square of mystery cheese barely clinging to a rogue corner of a wheat disc that disintegrated the moment I made eye contact with it. That was not a snack. That was a cry for help in cracker form.

I want a sample that makes me rethink everything.

That tastes like forgiveness.

That sings to me in a language I don't speak but emotionally understand.

And yes—Greg, if you're reading this: I'm sorry.

But also... WHERE WAS THE LOVE, GREG?

. . .

9. Music

Let's talk about the music.

There's a reason people wear sunglasses at night in Trader Joe's. And no—it's not just because half of us are in the witness protection program and the other half are trying to avoid an ex who works in produce. That's only, like, part of it.

The real reason?

Because the music in your store is a full-blown emotional ambush.

I came in for frozen dumplings.

Next thing I know, "Danny's Song" starts playing, and suddenly I'm sobbing in front of the organic lentils like someone just read me my childhood diary out loud.

You don't play music—you weaponize nostalgia.

You drop Loggins and Messina like emotional napalm.

You fire off "Listen to the Music" and suddenly every forty-something in the store is swaying like they're at Woodstock but with almond flour.

By the time Fleetwood Mac comes on, I'm whispering, "I miss you, Mom," into a head of romaine.

There's a woman openly slow dancing with a watermelon.

The cashier is crying, but still smiling, because that's the Trader Joe's way.

I don't know who curates this playlist, but I assume it's a retired therapist with a vendetta and access to vinyl.

So yes, your store is cozy. Yes, it smells like roasted garlic and forgiveness.

But if one more emotionally loaded banger from 1977 hits while I'm trying to compare yogurt brands, I swear I will fall to my knees in front of the refrigerated hummus and relive every failed relationship I've ever had—through song.

Please... give us a warning.

Or a support group.

Or at least tissues at the sample table.

10. Plants

Let's talk about the plant section—Trader Joe's unofficial jungle of emotional triggers.

I walked in for oat milk and walked out with a potted succulent named Mike.

Mike now lives in my apartment. Mike has better lighting than I do. Mike is thriving while I spiral.

I don't know how it happened. One minute I was in frozen foods, the next I was justifying a $5.99 houseplant as a coping mechanism.

Your little jungle is not "charming." It's a botanical trap.

Each fern whispers, *Buy me. You'll be the kind of person who remembers to water things.*

Lies.

I now have five plants. Two are on life support.

One is hanging from the shower curtain rod like a damp emotional hostage.

Stop luring emotionally vulnerable people into relationships with underpriced fiddle leaf figs.

We came for groceries, not a chlorophyll-coded midlife crisis.

Oh, we're closing this thing out with full-blown soundtrack-of-your-therapy-era energy—where every sentence feels like it's been emotionally scored by a classic rock radio station and a crying jukebox.

In Closing

And so I say—with trembling fingers and a cart full of gluten-free regret—

"Like a bridge over troubled water...I will lay me down." Right there. On the linoleum. Next to the unsweetened almond milk.

"Baby come back..." This isn't just about Chicken Tikka Masala.

This is about trust. And fiber.

"You can't always get what you want..." But I'd like to at least get one box of Root Beer Float popsicles before Tyler, age seventeen, Venmos my last shred of dignity.

"Dream on..." Yes, Steven Tyler. I *will* dream on.

About a world where parking is fair, free samples are healing, and Cookie Butter returns my texts. And if this letter means nothing to you, if it gets thrown out like a soggy cauliflower gnocchi sample...

Just know this:

"I will survive." But only barely. And only with snacks.

Yours in deli section devotion,

Zapplewick, Q.

(Writing this from a lawn chair I've set up outside the freezer aisle. I'm not leaving. Not until the bell rings three times... and someone plays "Peaceful Easy Feeling.")

THREE LESSONS (like you needed more):

1. Never trust a bell you didn't ring. Especially when it sounds like it's summoning either help...or judgment. At Trader Joe's, it might be both.

2. Nostalgia is a gateway condiment. You came for hummus. You left with tears, a houseplant named Mike, and emotional whiplash from "Dreams" by Fleetwood Mac. It's fine. You're growing.

3. We're all hungry for something deeper. Sometimes it's Chicken Tikka Masala. Sometimes it's a healing sample that whispers you are loved in cheese form. But every aisle —if you're paying attention—is asking the same question:

What if someone truly saw you, the real you, the questioning, seeking you... and still offered you grace, answers and love?

— Stay Groovy

22

VW VAN

(OR HOW I ACCIDENTALLY PRACTICED MEDICINE WITHOUT A LICENSE)

There was a time I lived in a van. Not because I didn't have options—but because I had optimism, which, in my case, was just ambition without adult supervision.

It was a VW camper van, but let's not get romantic. It didn't have running water, a fridge, or stove. I cooked eggs on a backpack stove, ate peanut butter out of the jar, and treated raisins like a luxury item. I wasn't off the grid—I *was* a one-man survival documentary with no camera crew and suspicious hygiene.

The engine had all the horsepower of a squirrel's bicep. Uphill, I got overtaken by cyclists...on *unicycles.* I didn't "pass" other cars. I just hoped they felt charitable and moved over.

Cruise control? Sure. If by cruise control, you mean wedging a three-iron on the gas pedal while your legs stretch diagonally across the console. Then yeah, it had it.

I parked in the hospital lot where I worked. Yes—*worked.* As in "employed." As in "definitely should not have been." This was back when background checks weren't even a vibe.

And yes, that technically made me the original Trapper John. Except their vans were motorhomes, and their medical degrees were, you know, real. I was more like a *Disorderly Orderly*. Think Jerry Lewis in scrubs—with less coordination and more liability.

It all started when I ran out of money in Newport Beach. (Shocking, I know—turns out sunburns, smoothies, and beachfront rent don't pay for themselves.) I drifted inland, slightly crispy and fully broke, and wandered into a small, one-story acute care hospital. Sixty beds. Zero plan.

I asked about a job. The HR person talked to me for five minutes, said, "Come back after lunch," and I assumed I was still being interviewed. I wasn't. Turns out "come back after lunch" meant "clock in and start wiping things."

Apparently, they hired me because they needed someone large enough to lift patients. They weren't looking for experience. They were looking for mass. I was less "skilled " and more "a forklift with a pulse."

I was given scrubs and assigned patients. Let me repeat: *assigned patients*. With no training. No background. I walked into rooms like, "Hi, I'm Bob. This is my first day as a human."

The medical terms came at me fast. NPO? I thought it was a union. Q4? A droid in Star Wars. PRN? Thought it was a band. Turns out it just means "as needed." Like aspirin. Or common sense.

CHF? I guessed "Can't Handle Fluids." CVA? "Carefully Verify Appendages." COPD? "Consider Ordering Pizza, Dave."

Thankfully, I didn't hand out meds. There were real nurses for that. I was the guy who showed up with a chart, a confused smile, and a general sense of wonder that anyone had let me indoors.

There were...moments.

I'd show up, clipboard in hand, and casually ask which guy in the room ordered the enema—like it was a joke. It wasn't. Then I'd read the instructions like it was the first time I'd ever done it... because it *was* the first time I'd ever done it.

At one point, I even tried to casually ask the patient how *he* remembered it being done last time. You know—for "consistency." Truth was, I had no clue. I was one wrong move away from losing my job, my dignity, and possibly the respect of the entire gastrointestinal community.

Then there was the woman in restraints—sweet as pie, calm as a cat in the sun—who somehow convinced a doctor she didn't need to be tied down anymore. "She's alert, oriented, appropriate," he said confidently. "Let's give her some dignity."

We exchanged the kind of look that says, *Sir... this is not your best idea.* But he had the badge, the degree, and the rank, so we untied her.

Thirty seconds later—*bonk*—she clocked him right in the head with her cast like it was a hammer, and he was the nail. You could hear the hollow thud echo down the hallway. He blinked. We blinked. She smiled.

We didn't say, "I told you so." We just nodded respectfully to the unconscious wisdom of the moment, stuffed our laughter into our scrub pockets, and gently re-tied the restraints like it was part of the care plan all along.

Or there was Houdini. Not her real name, obviously—but the only one that fit after what she pulled. She convinced a brand-new nurse—bless her optimistic little heart—to loosen her restraints. "Just a little more comfort, sweetheart," Houdini cooed. "I promise I'll behave."

Five minutes later? Gone.

Picture this: you're pulling into the hospital to visit Grandma, holding a balloon and a card, when a barefoot woman in a hospital gown sprints across the parking lot like she's chasing Olympic gold.

Behind her? A nurse and myself yelling, "WHICH WAY DID SHE GO?" Visitors pointed.

We finally caught her. We walked her back inside just in time for the doctor to round the corner, clipboard in hand, utterly unaware he had nearly missed the hospital's first 100-yard dash patient.

Meals? If a patient got discharged before lunch, well, there may or may not have been a systematic and entirely unregulated redistribution of Salisbury steaks. (I cannot legally confirm this. My lawyer twitches when I do.)

Showers? I learned the rhythm of surgeries and timed mine accordingly—slipping into the doctors' locker room while they were knee-deep in laparoscopic procedures. It was a delicate dance: They removed gallbladders; I lathered Head & Shoulders. Everyone had a role. Eight minutes in, eight minutes out. Any longer, and I risked a very awkward encounter with someone licensed to operate heavy machinery on human organs. It was stealth hygiene at its best—like Navy SEALs, but with Irish Spring and questionable credentials.

Eventually, I blended in. Scrubs helped. Confidence helped more. Walk like you belong, and no one asks questions—especially if you're holding a chart.

One day, I casually asked a surgeon if I could observe a procedure. He shrugged and said, "Sure." Probably thought I was a med student. I wasn't. I was a glorified furniture mover with a stethoscope.

I stood by the table hoping not to pass out. My greatest fear was not blood—it was that the surgeon would look at me and say, "You wanna close?"

When the charge nurse asked where I was and I told her, she freaked out. Big time. "You're *where*? Doing *what*? With *who*?"

Apparently, "hanging out in the OR" wasn't in my job description. But then, neither was *anything* I'd been doing, but up until that point, no one had asked.

Eventually—gradually—I learned. I picked up the terminology, figured out how to take vitals, and got just close enough to the world of medicine to realize something important: the passion to make it happen just wasn't there. And honestly? I'm thankful for that. Important life lesson learned early—before anyone let me near a scalpel.

I moved on to other callings—other kinds of healing. Ministry came next. Fewer stethoscopes, more soul work. Still messy. Still holy. Just with fewer acronyms... and fewer Salisbury steaks. And yes, I eventually upgraded from the van.

THREE THINGS I took away from my van life experience:

1. Never underestimate the power of a peanut butter jar and a golf club. These are the unsung heroes of van life, emergency cruise control, and protein.

2. Scrubs are like capes. If you wear them with confidence, no one asks questions. Until you faint in the OR. Then they ask a lot of questions.

3. God doesn't wait for you to have it all together. He meets you in parking lots, hospitals, vans—and all the in-between places where life feels uncertain. He calls nobodies and gives them somebodies to love. Even if they don't know what NPO means. So ask yourself: Where is God meeting you? The answer might come with a lesson you didn't expect—but probably need.

— Stay Groovy

23

DAVE

Forgiveness and healing are not the same.

They're related—sometimes inseparably—but they're not synonymous. Forgiveness restores your standing before God; healing restores your soul. One is instantaneous. The other is often painstaking. Forgiveness is declared. Healing is walked out.

Forgiveness is positional.

Yes, it can bring peace. Yes, it can be felt. But at its core, forgiveness is a radical, even *cosmic* shift in our relationship with God. It's God placing our sin on Jesus—and placing Jesus's righteousness on us.

It happens the moment we trust in Christ's atoning work and resurrection.

Not merely that He died, but that He died *for us.* That His death was substitutional. That He bore our sins in His body on the cross so we could die to sin and live to righteousness (1 Peter 2:24). Forgiveness is a spiritual rebirth—once for all time.

Healing, on the other hand, is how we learn to walk in the newness that forgiveness provides.

And healing—especially emotional healing—also comes from Jesus. But more often than not, He delivers it through His body: the

Church, not just through sermons or Sunday services, but through the gritty grace of a few faithful people who show up in your life. People who see you, hear you, and stay.

For me, that group was the first church I attended as a new believer.

It didn't just become a place I went—it became the home I didn't know I was missing. I didn't have words for it at the time, but every time I walked through those doors, it felt like coming home. Not because of the building—but because of the belonging.

God began to knit my soul back together there. Not with lightning bolts or miracle moments—but with shared meals, chaotic potlucks, and the quiet constancy of people who kept showing up.

Sometimes healing doesn't come through a crowd—it comes through one person. One conversation. One example. One life quietly poured out.

For me, that person was Dave.

Dave was one of the pastors at the church I had started attending. But that title doesn't begin to capture who he was in my life. Dave loved with the kind of love that's honest, soul-deep, and utterly without pretense.

The kind David expressed for Jonathan in his famous eulogy: "Your love was more wonderful than that of women" (2 Samuel 1:26).

It wasn't sexual. It certainly wasn't inappropriate. It was the kind of love an orphaned heart craves—the kind more men need than would ever dare to admit.

It was foundational love.

The kind that steadies you. Grounds you. Prepares you. The kind that says: *You matter. You belong. You're safe here. You can grow here.*

In Dave's case, that love wasn't loud or sentimental. It wasn't hugs and heart-to-hearts. It showed up in a handshake that said, *You're seen*, and a smile that made it safe to exhale. It showed up in chaotic dinners at his house—kids shouting, dishes clattering, a dachshund named Sydney barking at everything that moved. But even the noise was healing. Because it wasn't the sterile, dysfunctional chaos I'd grown up with. It was holy chaos. Loud but loving.

Messy but warm. Grace-soaked disorder where love always had the last word.

Dave introduced me to weekly rhythms that reshaped my soul. We met regularly. He didn't start with performance or theology. He started with a simple, disarming question: "How is your soul?" You might think I coined that phrase. I didn't. It came from Dave.

He modeled transparency. Accountability. Manhood—not as bravado, but as integrity. He led annual camping trips to Havasu Falls, where we memorized Scripture, carried others' burdens (and backpacks), and learned how to serve without needing to be noticed.

At church, I saw Dave the shepherd—wise and grounded.

At home, I saw Dave, the dad, present and patient in the middle of chaos.

On the trail, I saw Dave, my friend—sweaty, fun, unfiltered, and kind.

And in all of it, I saw Jesus—healing me through Dave.

There were others too. Steve taught me how to plant a church. Rocky showed me what a pastor's heart looked like. But Dave was the backstory that made it all make sense.

His laugh came from someplace deep—like joy had roots in him.

And his prayers? They didn't sound rehearsed or religious. They were soaked in belief, saturated in Scripture, and spoken like he actually knew the One he was talking to. He didn't perform prayers. He prayed. And just being near him when he did felt like healing.

~

If I've learned anything, it's this:

1. Be a Dave. Just show up in someone's life and be who you are in Christ. You don't need a title or a platform. Just take a walk. Ask a question. Invite someone into your holy chaos. Invest in someone who's already hoping for you—whether they say it out loud or not because it's what He wants to do with every follower of Jesus. There is nothing

more fulfilling than being part of someone's healing story. This world is full of people who need healing—and just as full of people called to be healers. Not perfect ones. Not all-knowing experts. Just real people who are willing to show up, stay awhile, and love. You don't have to have all the answers. You just have to *be there.* Healing happens along the way. And sometimes, all someone needs is your life to say: *You're not alone. God sees you. And He sent me to remind you.*

2. Thank your Dave. Let him (or her) know they were part of your healing. Although if they truly are a Dave, they probably already know. Here's mine: *You showed up. You listened. You prayed like you meant it. You welcomed me into a holy kind of chaos—the kind that healed parts of me I didn't even know were broken. Thank you for being that person. For me, and for many others. You didn't just teach truth—you lived it. And through that, Jesus met me. I'll never forget it.*

— Stay Groovy

24

1984

Maybe you've heard of this little athletic event coming to America in a few years.

It's called the Olympics.

Thinking about what's coming in 2028 made me flash back to the last time Los Angeles hosted the Games—1984, a glorious summer of international excellence, peak athleticism, and... personal social disasters.

Yes, the big-ticket events took place at the Coliseum, where champions were crowned and history was made.

But the rest of the events?

Scattered like spare change across Southern California.

And to my complete shock—you could actually get tickets. So naturally, I went to a few.

Let's take a tour of my Olympic experience, which included:

Scorching heat.

Misidentified sports.

And a dating strategy so flawed it should've been an Olympic event itself.

. . .

Women's Field Hockey

Yep. That's what I chose.

Held at East Los Angeles College in Monterey Park—where the sun apparently lives.

Here's what I remember:

It was hot. I mean, "bake-a-lasagna-on-your-forehead" hot.

The teams were Australia and... um... Not Australia.

I knew absolutely nothing about field hockey. Still don't.

I attended with a girl whose name I never learned.

Yes. That actually happened.

How did we meet?

At school, I saw her and said, "Hey, wanna go to an Olympic event Saturday?"

She said yes.

I said: "Cool. I'll pick you up here at ten."

That was the entire exchange.

No name. No number. No common sense.

When it came to dating, I was as smooth as gravel in a blender.

We sat together, silently sizzling in the Monterey Park sun, surrounded by nineteen die-hard fans of women's field hockey and one guy who thought it was probably just "grass hockey, but with skirts."

And still—I never asked her name.

Here's the thing: the longer you wait, the more awkward it becomes.

By the second half, we were in the full "too-late-to-ask" Twilight Zone.

I kept trying to think of a clever workaround: "So... do you spell that with an 'E' or a 'Y'?"

She just looked at me, furrowed brow, "Neither."

Clearly, dating was not my strong suit.

Needless to say, the relationship didn't survive the parking lot.

If you're reading this now—sorry. I was young, clueless, and dehydrated.

. . .

Men's Marathon

This one was genuinely cool.

I watched it with my buddy Pat—a friend whose name I *did* know, thank you very much.

We watched the start on TV, then jumped in the car, raced to San Vicente Boulevard, watched them jog by in person, then rushed home to catch the TV finish.

I remember standing near a hydration station—a long table lined with clearly labeled bottles, like an Olympic juice bar run by obsessive-compulsive interns.

As the runners passed, I was struck by how they all looked less like elite athletes and more like determined flamingos. Arms flailing. Legs spinning. But they were flying.

After the last runner passed, I convinced Pat to take staged photos of me grabbing a water bottle and looking dramatically exhausted.

Honestly? Pretty convincing.

And very fun.

Pat, if you have those pics, I'd love to see them.

Men's Handball

Let's clear something up.

This was not the kind of handball I knew growing up—the one with concrete walls, a rubber ball, and a bruised ego.

No, Olympic handball is a whole other beast. Think:

Water polo.

Minus the water.

Plus jetpacks.

I only went because tickets were available, and my standards were somewhere between "Why not?" and "How bad could it be?"

Answer:

It was incredible.

Here's how it works:

You pass a ball the size of a grapefruit.

No dribbling. No stepping into the forbidden zone.

And when it's go-time, one guy leaps into the air, floats like Neo from *The Matrix*, and fires the ball past the goalie before gravity remembers he exists.

These guys were hovering.

One dude stayed in the air long enough to file his taxes.

I was sitting right behind the goal, with a perfect view.

No date. No name to forget.

Just me and some dudes—and the unspoken male agreement that we didn't need to remember each other's names anyway.

"Bro" works just fine.

Baseball at Dodger Stadium

This was a doubleheader.

Game 1: Nicaragua vs. Canada.

Result: I forget. I remember heat, boredom, and a lot of polite clapping.

Possibly the only Olympic event where someone in the crowd fell asleep *during* a home run.

Game 2: Korea vs. Japan.

Completely different universe.

There were flags. There were drums and chants.

There were guys in the stands who clearly trained for this moment.

Every cheer was synchronized, every movement rehearsed.

I half expected someone to hold up scorecards for crowd enthusiasm.

I didn't know who to root for, so I just cheered for whoever had the louder fans.

Bonus: I went with a girl named Cathy.

I was learning.

Laura's Olympic Experience

Years later, I met Laura—the woman I would eventually marry.

We started comparing Olympic stories.

She went to all the prime events at the Coliseum, naturally.

With ridiculously attractive guys.

(That part was unnecessary to mention, but thank you for the emotional damage.)

She said she sat at the finish line.

I said I sat in the outer ring of the sun watching mystery girl and mystery sport.

She remembered a race where a woman fell.

I said, "Mary Decker."

She remembered a guy who was really fast.

I said, "Carl Lewis."

She said, "Yes! That's him! He was fast, *and* he could jump really far."

I said, "Yep—four golds. Total legend."

Then she asked, "What did you see?"

I said, "Women's field hockey."

She asked, "Who did you go with?"

I said, "I don't know."

She laughed and said, "It's okay. We're married now."

And I said, "No. Really. I *never* knew her name."

Pause.

She squinted at me. "Wait... you went to an Olympic event, sat through the whole thing, drove her home... and never asked her name?"

"Yup," I said. "That about sums it up."

She turned away, "Huh," she muttered. Not mad. Not amused. Just... recalculating.

Honestly?

One more reason I'm glad we're married now.

Because if it was the audition tape, I wouldn't have gotten a call back.

THREE LIFE LESSONS (Brought to You by 1984 and Mild Heatstroke)

1. Never wait too long to ask someone's name. By the second quarter of field hockey, you've passed the socially acceptable "Hi, what's your name?" window and entered the "I guess we're just strangers sweating silently together" zone. Pro tip: If you're already sharing sunblock and still don't know her name, it's too late.

2. If your Olympic strategy includes "just pick whatever still has tickets, you might end up watching grown men throw a grapefruit at a net while pretending to fly. And you will love it.

3. Some of the best things happen when you stop pretending to know what's going on. We all want to be known. Not just cheered for when we win—but seen, even when we're awkward, anonymous, or melting in the stands. The good news? There's One who already knows your name. You don't have to impress Him, memorize the rules, or make the final cut. He's seen you at your worst and invites you in anyway.

— Stay Groovy

25

RORY

Our dog died last week.

We had him for fourteen human years—which, as every third-grader with a calculator can tell you, is ninety-eight in dog years. That's basically Gandalf status. If Rory had opposable thumbs and a long beard, he could've led us through Mordor, stopped for snacks, and still made it back in time for dinner.

He died of old age. We saw it coming. The signs were everywhere—hearing loss, fading eyesight, tremors, unsteady legs, and bladder issues. Again, to clarify: we're still talking about *the dog*, not me. Although, give me a couple more birthdays and that distinction may get blurrier.

And yet—even knowing the end was near—it still hit hard. You think you're ready. You rehearse your response, like it's a school play. But real grief doesn't follow scripts. When that final breath leaves their furry little body, the silence that follows is louder than anything you've ever heard. No paws padding across the hardwood. No heavy sighs as he settles into his favorite nap position. Just a void where faithfulness used to sleep.

I had to be the one to tell Laura.

I'd mentally rehearsed it—several times, actually. In my head I was calm, kind, maybe even poetic. In reality, I just stood there like a malfunctioning Roomba, bumping into emotional furniture. Rehearsals, it turns out, are the lies we tell ourselves to pretend we're prepared for life.

When I told her, she froze. Like someone had unplugged her from the wall. And then she cried—the kind of cry that shakes your body like a storm, the kind that doesn't ask your permission. She cried all day. And then some.

Rory was a special dog. I liked him. But Laura—Laura *loved* him. I'm not really an animal guy. If I had to rank my enthusiasm for pets, I'd put it somewhere between flossing and folding fitted sheets. But if you had to have a dog—and I did—Rory was the one you'd want. Gentle. Unfailingly loyal. Weirdly intuitive. It was like he took a solemn vow in an invisible dog chapel: "For better or for worse, through kibble and through canned food, till death do us part."

He was Laura's untrained emotional support dog. Though if you watched him work, you'd swear he had a master's in clinical psychology. No credentials, but all the instincts. When depression hit Laura hard—when the bed was her only refuge—Rory stayed put. No barking. No pacing. Just quiet presence. That tail-thump of solidarity. That warm body at her bedside to say, "I'm here. We'll wait this out together."

I used to joke that we should've named him Shadow. Because he followed her *everywhere*. To the bathroom? Yep. To the kitchen? Naturally. To the mailbox? Absolutely. Once, she stepped outside for thirty seconds to throw something in the trash, and Rory stood watch at the back door like she'd boarded the Titanic. He didn't budge. If she left through the front door, he waited at the front. Side door? He moved to the side. He was like a one-man welcome committee with separation anxiety.

He had rhythm too. He knew our routines better than *we* did. At night, we'd turn off the TV, and the moment he heard the *click*, he'd trot to the door like it was a stage cue. Showtime. Business time. Pavlov was proud. Actually, *we* were Pavlov's dogs. Rory trained *us*.

And then...there was the cat incident.

One afternoon, Rory saw a stray cat wander into our backyard. I let him out, and in a flash, this aging, limping, blurry-eyed relic of a creature transformed into a greyhound with a grudge. He launched himself like a cannonball across the yard. We were stunned. It was like watching your ninety-five-year-old grandpa pole vault.

The next day, I found that same cat—lifeless—in the alley. I have no idea what happened. Old age? Gang dispute? Divine feline judgment? All I know is, there was Rory, back at the window, watching. Waiting. You ever try to explain death to a dog? "Buddy… the cat's not coming back." He just kept staring out the glass like, *It'll be back. Cats always come back.* Loyal to a fault.

And then there were the sirens. Just when we began to wonder if Rory was secretly part human—like maybe we'd accidentally adopted a wizard trapped in dog form—he'd remind us he was all canine by howling at fire engine sirens. Not police cars. Not ambulances. Only fire engines. He had standards.

Not that I haven't felt the urge to howl at a fire truck myself. Especially during tax season.

Then there was the night our neighbor earned himself a place in the Rory Hall of Fame. We pulled into the alley behind our house and saw him out there, pacing with a flashlight like he was auditioning for a crime docuseries.

"What are you looking for?" I asked.

"I heard moaning," he said, eyes wide. "Like someone was hurt. Or dying."

It was Rory.

He was in our backyard—alive and well—but wailing like the final act of a Shakespeare play. In dog-language, he was crying out: *I have been abandoned! Left alone in the shadows! For five entire dog years! Will no one call the authorities?*

In reality, we'd been gone for forty-five minutes. He had food. He had water. He had mood lighting. But no Laura. And that, to him, was unforgivable.

It's the little things you miss. The click of his nails on the tile. The soft thud as he plopped down beside Laura. The way he'd rest his chin on her knee at breakfast, like a living bookmark. Or that peculiar half-sneeze, half-bark noise he made when he wanted attention but didn't want to *look* like he wanted attention. Prideful little manipulator.

Losing him didn't just disrupt our routines—it dislocated something in our hearts. He wasn't just a dog. He was a presence. A memory-keeper. A companion in the quietest and loudest chapters of our lives.

And Laura? She's still grieving. Honestly, so am I. We both are. Maybe that's the bargain we make when we invite animals into our lives. We give them our hearts, knowing they'll eventually break them. But somehow, it's still worth it. Every tail wag. Every ridiculous fetch. Every moment they made us laugh when we didn't think we could.

Rory didn't just love us. He *taught* us how to love. To show up. To wait by the door. To follow close. To care deeply without needing words.

Rest well, Rory.

You never asked for anything.

But you gave us everything.

~

LESSONS? Of course.

1. Never underestimate the power of routine—or a remote control. Rory was a creature of habit. One click of the TV remote, and he was up like clockwork, ready for his nightly business. Honestly, he had better instincts than most smart home systems. If only he'd figured out how to make coffee.

2. Sometimes the greatest comfort comes from someone who says nothing at all. Rory never offered advice. Never tried to fix anything. He just stayed—close and quiet—

especially on Laura's hardest days. He knew that presence can be more healing than words. That kind of loyalty doesn't bark. It just stays.

3. He waited by the door she left through—because he believed she'd return. That's faith. Faith looks like watching, hoping, staying near the place where reunion might happen. Rory believed the one he loved would come back. And maybe that's how we're meant to live—eyes on the door, heart expectant, waiting for the One we love to return.

— Stay Groovy

CLOSING THOUGHTS

Dear Reader,

Thank you for reading. Stories come alive when they're shared, and I'm so grateful you shared your time with these. My prayer is that something here encouraged you, made you pause, or moved you a little nearer to hope. Your attention is a gift I don't take lightly.

With gratitude,

R.W. Wesley

Want to know more about Jesus?

Check out these creative presentations: https://www.greatcommission.com/believe.html

Want to know how to make disciples?

Practical resources and simple, reproducible steps are waiting for you at: greatcommission.com

AI Disclaimer

This book was written with the help of artificial intelligence. Think of AI as a tireless assistant—one that never needs a coffee break and doesn't complain about long hours. While AI helped polish grammar and readability, the story, plot, tone, and arc remain fully human—shaped by the imagination, experience, and heart of the author. The robots are not taking over... at least not yet.

ALSO BY R.W. WESELY

If you enjoyed this book, you may also like:

- *Detective Penny: Some Evidence Leads to Justice, Some Whispers Your Name—book 1.*
- *Detective Penny: Some Truths Set You Free, Some Make You Disappear—book 2.*
- *Pulsers – Mystery Spreads, Fear Surges, Justice Wavers.*
- *Seven Questions That Are Changing the World: Discovering Hope, Belonging, and Purpose.*

Did you know there's a free five-week discussion guide for Stay Groovy?

You can download it anytime at **www.GreatCommission.com**.

It's a great fit for book clubs or small groups looking for a fresh, story-driven way to spark meaningful conversation—whether you're exploring faith, friendship, or the deeper purpose behind everyday life.

The discussion guide is also an ideal on-ramp for those who want to create a safe, welcoming space where unchurched friends and neighbors can gather, laugh, and talk about life in a fun, creative way.

EPILOGUE

I'd seen him before.

Not just once. Several times.

He never looked past me like the others did. Never sneered or rolled his eyes.

Jesus always noticed me—even though I did everything I could to blend into the back of the crowd.

I was there in the house the day He healed that paralyzed man. I remember the way Jesus spoke. The way He forgave.

The way He silenced the religious elite with a single sentence: "Which is easier—to say your sins are forgiven, or to say, 'Get up and walk'?"

And then the man stood up.

Just like that.

No delay. No drama.

Forgiveness and healing. Soul and body.

I went home with a question that day I couldn't shake:

What if he could do the same for me?

I didn't deserve it.

I knew what I was.

A traitor. A tax collector.

A man who earned well, yes—but at a cost.

I'd tell myself I was just doing my job, that the markup the Romans demanded wasn't my fault.

But that didn't ease the hatred I saw in people's eyes.

I was the target they felt safe hating—because I didn't carry a sword.

What they didn't see was that I hated it too.

The distance. The loneliness.

The way guilt eats away at a man until he starts to believe he's nothing more than the worst thing he's ever done.

I felt hollow.

Like something inside me was dying.

So when Jesus approached my booth that day, I froze.

He wasn't just passing by.

He was coming for me.

He stopped, locked eyes with me, and said two words:

"Follow me."

No lecture. No shame. No conditions.

Just a call.

Something shifted in that moment.

I stood up—left everything behind—and followed him.

It was like trading in a lead cloak for air.

Guilt for grace.

Isolation for belonging.

A half-life for real life.

I didn't know what the future held, but I knew who I'd be walking with.

And I knew one thing for sure: I had to tell others.

Even the ones I didn't really trust.

Even the ones who didn't trust me.

So I threw a dinner.

Not a networking event. Not a religious seminar.

Just food, and Jesus, and people like me who needed what He offered.

We sat around the table, eating and laughing and listening to this

Rabbi who didn't talk like anyone else.

And for the first time in years, I didn't feel like I was performing.

I felt... seen. Known. Clean.

Of course, the criticism came.

Whispers. Looks. Raised eyebrows from the righteous.

"How can he eat with *them*?" they said.

But Jesus wasn't rattled.

He looked right at them and said,

"It's not the healthy who need a doctor, but the sick.

I haven't come to call the righteous, but sinners."

And I knew:

He was talking about me.

And for the first time in my life, that didn't sting.

It healed.

GOD SENT Jesus into the world to say, "I know you." He knows the choices that haunt you. The words you regret—and the ones you wish you had the courage to say. He knows the spiral of thoughts that wear you down, the grief that clings, the shame that whispers, *You're not enough.*

And he's not running from any of it. He's running toward you because you were never created to carry such a heavy weight.

He was.

Jesus doesn't just offer a second chance—He offers rest. The real kind. The soul-deep kind. Not just a fresh start, but a whole new life.

And just like Matthew, maybe today is your day to get up and follow Him. Not perfectly. Just honestly.

He'll take it from there.

"COME TO ME, all who are weary and burdened, and I will give you rest."
—Jesus (Matthew 11:28)

Made in the USA
Las Vegas, NV
03 November 2025

33343352R00081